Walpole and the Whig Supremacy

WALPOLE
and the Whig Supremacy

H. T. Dickinson

The English Universities Press Ltd

ISBN 0 340 11515 7

The English Universities Press Ltd
St Paul's House, Warwick Lane, London EC4P 4AH
Printed in Great Britain by Hazell Watson & Viney Ltd
Aylesbury, Bucks

Introduction to the Series

This series has been undertaken in the conviction that there can be no subject of study more important than history. Great as have been the conquests of natural science in our time – such that many think of ours as a scientific age *par excellence* – it is even more urgent and necessary that advances should be made in the social sciences, if we are to gain control of the forces of nature loosed upon us. The bed out of which all the social sciences spring is history; there they find, in greater or lesser degree, subject-matter and material, verification or contradiction.

There is no end to what we can learn from history, if only we will, for it is coterminous with life. Its special field is the life of man in society, and at every point we can learn vicariously from the experience of others before us in history.

To take one point only – the understanding of politics: how can we hope to understand the world of affairs around us if we do not know how it came to be what it is? How to understand Germany, or Soviet Russia, or the United States – or ourselves, without knowing something of their history?

There is no subject that is more useful, or indeed indispensable.

Some evidence of the growing awareness of this may be seen in the immense increase in the interest of the reading public in history and the much larger place this subject has come to take in education in our time.

This series has been planned to meet the needs and demands of a very wide public and of education – they are indeed the same. I am convinced that the most congenial, as well as the most concrete and practical, approach to history is the biographical, through the lives of the great men whose actions have been so much part of history, and whose careers in turn have been so moulded and formed by events.

The key idea of this series, and what distinguishes it from any other that has appeared, is the intention by way of a biography of a great man to open up a significant historical theme: for example, Cromwell and the Puritan Revolution, or Lenin and the Russian Revolution.

My hope is, in the end, as the series fills out and completes itself, by a sufficient number of biographies to cover whole periods and subjects in that way. To give you the history of the United States, for example, or the British Empire or France, *via* a number of biographies of their leading historical figures.

That should be something new, as well as convenient and practical, in education.

I need hardly say that I am a strong believer in people with good academic standards writing once more for the general reading public, and of the public being given the best that the universities can provide. From this point of view this series is intended to bring the university into the homes of the people.

A. L. R O W S E
All Souls College, Oxford

Contents

Plates

Acknowledgements

The author and publisher wish to thank the following for per-
mission to reproduce the illustrations in this book : the British
Museum, plates I, VI, VII, VIII, IX, X; the National Portrait
Gallery, plates II, III, IV, V.

Preface

Although he was the most successful British politician of the eighteenth century, there is no modern, single-volume life of Sir Robert Walpole. The best available biographies are William Coxe's old study, *Memoirs of the Life and Administration of Sir Robert Walpole* (3 vols., 1798) and J. H. Plumb's uncompleted work, *Sir Robert Walpole* (2 vols., 1956, 1960). This short work cannot match the detail of these two studies. Moreover, although it is based on original research, it does not offer any important new evidence or any radically different interpretation. It does, however, attempt a deeper analysis of the major achievements of Walpole's career. It seeks in particular to explain how Walpole did more than any other politician to safeguard the Hanoverian succession, the Revolution Settlement, and the Whig supremacy.

There are no footnotes, but all the important sources are listed in the bibliography. The sources of the few quotations used have usually been identified in the text. Those from Walpole's speeches in the House of Commons are taken from William Cobbett's *Parliamentary History of England*.

My wife assisted me at every stage in the preparation of this work. Frances Dow read an earlier draft with the greatest care and the final text has benefited a great deal from her shrewd advice.

HARRY DICKINSON
Edinburgh University 1972

For my mother and father

I Walpole and the Whigs

FAMILY

Robert Walpole was to become the most able political manager of the eighteenth century, his techniques and methods copied by all the successful ministers of Hanoverian Britain. Yet he started life with only the minimum of social advantages necessary to bring him within the bounds of the political nation. His social background and his economic circumstances were sufficiently favourable to allow him to embark on a career in public life, but not substantial enough to lead any of his contemporaries to predict a great political future for him.

Walpole was born into a fairly prosperous and well-established county family of the type which dominated the House of Commons of his day, but he was not a powerful aristocrat who could expect to be consulted when major political decisions were being made. Both his father and his grandfather had sufficient social standing and political influence to sit in Parliament, though neither had made their mark in national affairs. His father, the elder Robert Walpole, was a man of intelligence, ambition, and strength of purpose, who laid the foundations of the family's future greatness. A widely-read, even scholarly man, he was also a consummate man of business. He showed great enterprise in managing his modest estates and he was among those improving Norfolk landowners who adopted the Dutch methods of farming in the late seventeenth century. He enclosed his land, improved the soil by marling, introduced new crops, particularly turnips and clover, and began to rotate his crops to avoid leaving part of his land fallow every year. The increased income from his estates was carefully husbanded and he spent only what was necessary to maintain his position as one of the leading squires of the county. His prudence and his ambition were inherited by his son, Robert, but, as the third son, young Robert Walpole did not expect to succeed to his father's estates or to follow him into Parliament. It was the deaths of his two elder brothers that rescued him from a career in the Church and the sudden demise of his father that allowed him to enter Parliament at an early age.

The younger Robert Walpole was born in the old family manor house at Houghton, in Norfolk, on 26 August 1676, but, after the age of six, he spent much of his time away from home, though he never lost his strong attachment to Houghton and to his family and neighbours. At six he was sent to be educated at a small school at Great Dunham, at thirteen he went on to Eton, and, in 1696, he went up to King's College, Cambridge. His academic studies were cut short after two years because the deaths of his two older brothers forced his father to call him back to Houghton to learn the business of estate management. His father's own health was very bad at this time and it showed no signs of improving. He was therefore anxious to see young Robert well established and well versed in his duties before he inherited the family estates. In 1699 he arranged the marriage of his son to Catherine Shorter, the daughter of a Baltic timber merchant from Kent. She brought with her a dowry of seven thousand pounds, which was largely spent discharging the mortgages on the Walpole estates. Catherine lacked her husband's self-control and her jealous, passionate nature made for a stormy marriage. At least in their first years together Robert Walpole returned her passion and both of them sought to enjoy life to the full, spending in the process far more than they could afford. Later, as their marriage became loveless, both of them sought consolation elsewhere. It is known that he kept several mistresses and fathered a number of illegitimate children. One of these relationships, with Maria Skerrett, lasted for years. He eventually married her in 1738, after the death of his first wife, but Maria died following a miscarriage later the same year. Catherine Walpole was not faithful either, and it is possible that her youngest son, the celebrated Horace Walpole, was not the child of her lawful husband, though Walpole was prepared to accept him as his son.

Robert Walpole's father died on 18 November 1700, leaving his heir a fairly prosperous estate, an established social position in the county, and the chance to embark on a political career. The new head of the family took advantage of this opportunity to play a greater role in social and political life, despite his lack of experience and the problem of supporting his mother, his two sisters and two younger brothers, as well as his own wife, who was expecting their first child. An ambitious man, who desired both wealth and power, he was clearly a young man in a hurry, but he did not lack foresight nor affection for his family. A strongly built and coarse-featured man, with dark hair and eyes, his character matched his appearance. All his life he showed that he had courage and an indomitable spirit, and that he was hard-working, resourceful, and clear-sighted. While he was extravagant and spent lavishly on food, wine, and material possessions, he also became renowned for his realism and his pragmatism, his hard-headed commonsense, and his sound judgement in business and politics. Although he desired and achieved great riches and high offices, he remained in many respects an unspoilt squire. One of his greatest joys was hunting, and in all his affairs he was invariably cheerful, affable, and approachable. He did not possess an elevated mind or profess high moral standards, but he was devoted to his family and friends, and he was unrivalled at persuading other people to share his opinions. While not always principled or even honest, he was always frank and straightforward, and managed to inspire trust in his judgement and confidence in his ability. His political success owed much to his engaging personal qualities and his great strength of character.

For some years before his father's death Robert Walpole had taken an interest in the management of the borough of Castle Rising, which his father had represented since 1689, and he had corresponded regularly with Thomas Howard, the other Member for the borough. Howard controlled the majority of the burgage votes, but he had been forced to come to terms

with the Walpole family, which had also built up a considerable influence in the borough. Howard and the elder Robert Walpole had agreed to share both the parliamentary representation
and the annual appointment of the mayor of the borough. The
younger Robert Walpole had helped to promote this accommodation and, within two days of his father's death, he was writing
to Howard to get him to continue the agreement so that he
could succeed to his father's seat in the Commons. In January
1701 Robert Walpole was chosen as one of the Members for
Castle Rising in the general election which had followed William
III's recent dissolution of Parliament.

Walpole had wisely decided that a political career afforded
the greatest opportunities for a man of ambition and talent who
wished to make his mark in the world. Following the Revolution
Settlement of 1689, Parliament at last became a permanent feature of the political scene. It was not only an annual assembly
for debating public affairs and passing the occasional, important
statute, but, following the financial innovations of the early
1690s, it effectively controlled the purse strings of the Government. As soon as he had been crowned King, William III had
brought England into the war he was waging against France.
The Government's need for huge sums of ready cash to meet
the costs of this war had initiated a far-reaching financial revolution. The most important innovation was the development of
a completely new system of public credit, the National Debt.
The Bank of England was launched in 1694 to raise long-term
loans for the Government, while Parliament accepted the need
to underwrite them by appropriating the yield of specific taxes
for the payment of the interest to the public creditors. The
Government no longer had to resort to desperate financial ex-
pedients in time of war, while Parliament was able to influence
the decisions of the executive as never before. Parliament had
found the way to make itself an indispensable partner of the
Government. At the same time, general elections were held regularly, and more seats were contested than at any other period
prior to the reform of Parliament in 1832. The increased power
of Parliament and the greater frequency of electoral contests

kept the political temperature and the national interest in politics at a very high level. Ambitious men, such as Walpole, who wanted to enhance their social prestige and who hoped to increase their political influence, and even perhaps their economic power, looked to a seat in Parliament as the shortest cut to these ends.

A seat in Parliament might also lead to much higher things: to office under the Crown. The Revolution Settlement had put some restrictions on the royal prerogative, while the growing costs of government, especially during wartime, had made the Crown dependent on Parliament for votes of supply, but the monarch remained at the very centre of political life. He still retained the initiative in policy-making and the power to appoint courtiers, ministers, and administrators in the departments of state. He also controlled a vast amount of patronage, including the creation of peers and bishops, the promotion of officers in the armed forces, and the awarding of government contracts. The Revolution Settlement may have asserted the power of Parliament, but some of its consequences, particularly the financial revolution and the long series of wars against France, were a powerful stimulus to new forms of wealth and power associated with the growth of the executive. A financial interest prospered by lending huge sums of money to the Government at favourable rates of interest, while there were also greater career opportunities in the much-expanded armed forces. Moreover, to raise the necessary taxation and to provide the vital supplies for the armed forces, the Government had to expand such administrative institutions as the Treasury, the revenue departments, and the Post Office. The expansion of the size of the administration and its increased expenditure offered the successful politician the chance of richer financial pickings, not always by honest means, and of greater political influence than could be attained merely by a seat in Parliament. Walpole was fully aware of these possibilities and was quite ready to take advantage of them.

The Revolution Settlement not only created greater political opportunities at Court and in Parliament, but also posed the serious political problem of how to get these two sources of power to work in harmony. Effective government was only possible if the political decisions taken at Court were accepted by a majority in Parliament. Many politicians soon realized that the ability to carry through the policies which they supported could only be gained by a combination of the favour of the Crown and the confidence of Parliament. This realization encouraged them to organize political parties in order to dominate the debates in Parliament, to make them appear indispensable to the monarch, and so to dictate the policies of the Government. It was this pursuit of personal ambition and this desire to force the Government to accept certain policies and principles that accounts for the survival of the differences between the Whig and Tory parties after they had combined to carry through the Revolution Settlement. When Walpole entered Parliament in 1701, the rivalry between Whigs and Tories was intense, over both personalities and policies, yet he had no hesitation about enlisting under the Whig banner.

Walpole's decision was not based on the expectation of gaining rapid political advancement, for the Tories were in the ascendant when he embarked on his parliamentary career; but, because he proved his loyalty to the party, he reaped a handsome reward in the age of the Whig supremacy after 1714. Three factors influenced his decision. Most of his personal connections were with other Whigs; the nature and organization of the Whig party appealed to his realism and self-interest; and he was evidently in sympathy with Whig principles and policies. Though his uncle Horatio became a Tory placeman, most of Walpole's family and friends were Whigs. His father had consistently supported the Whigs in the 1690s and had been the guardian of the young Viscount Townshend, who, like Robert Walpole and Robert's younger brother, Horatio, was to become a staunch Whig in Anne's reign. Walpole's closest friends in Norfolk, including Sir Charles Turner, Sir John Holland, Roger Townshend, William Feilding, Ash Windham, and Waller Bacon, were all Whigs. Almost as soon as Walpole entered Parliament he made friends with Lord Orford, and this brought him into contact with the established leaders of the Whig party, the Junto lords. Although Walpole, Townshend, and their Norfolk allies can be identified as a distinct group in Parliament, they almost always acted in concert with the main body of the party, the Junto Whigs. Walpole, moreover, was also on intimate terms with the rising generation of Whig leaders, such as James Stanhope, William Pulteney, Spencer Compton, and William Cavendish, later second Duke of Devonshire. As early as 1703 he was elected to the celebrated Whig Kit Cat Club and was acknowledged as one of the foremost Whig spokesmen in the Commons. Thus, he quickly established himself among the leaders of the Whig party, and he remained in this inner circle for the rest of his life.

The nature and organization of the Whig party appealed to the ambition and hard-headed realism of Walpole. The most conservative element in the political nation, the ordinary country squires, who were fearful of the economic consequences of the financial innovations of the 1690s and the Government's willingness to embark on major wars in Europe to curb the ambitions of France, tended to look to the Tories to defend their interests. Those social and economic groups who believed they could take advantage of the financial revolution, the change in foreign policy, and the growth of the executive were more inclined to support the Whigs. Successful merchants who prospered in the late seventeenth century when trade expanded rapidly were ready to invest in government funds and the increasing number of joint-stock companies. They also hoped to benefit from government contracts and from a colonial and commercial war against France. Successful landowners who had adopted the new farming techniques and methods of estate management welcomed the opportunity of augmenting their income by court appointments, careers in the administration, or service in the armed forces. Walpole himself was an improving landowner, whose extravagant tastes forced him to look for government office and wise financial and commercial investments to keep his head above water. Throughout his career in politics he bought up more land, lined his pockets with public money, was on the closest terms with the directors of the Bank of England, invested heavily, and even indulged in a little private smuggling. He was the epitome of the successful Whig, who took full advantage of all the economic opportunities of the post-Revolution era.

The Whig party was not only abreast of the economic advances of the age, whereas the Tories were afraid of them, but it was also the more highly organized party. It lacked, of course, the cohesion of a modern party, for most of its members owed their seats in Parliament to no other interest than their own social and economic influence. At times, indeed, it was riven by personal rivalries and divided over particular issues, but, in general, it held together in the pursuit of its major aims. Walpole recognized the political value of the party's organizational strength and supported its main political objectives. He was never much of a political theorist, and he was not much given to declaring his support for abstract political opinions, but his behaviour throughout his long career makes it clear that he accepted the basic tenets of the Whig cause. Although the pressure of political events forced him to equivocate on occasions, there can be no doubt that he was loyal to the major doctrines of a Revolution Whig. He rejected the principles of divine right and indefeasible hereditary succession, and accepted Parliament's right to alter the succession to the Crown in order to safeguard the Protestant Settlement. Thus, he never questioned William III's right to the throne, he never deviated from his support of the Hanoverian succession, and he never flirted with the idea of a Jacobite restoration. He also accepted the constitutional consequences of the Revolution Settlement: a limited monarchy balanced by a powerful Parliament. Like most Whigs he was loyal to the principle of religious toleration, at least as far as accepting the right of Protestant Dissenters to freedom of worship. In addition to upholding these doctrines, he also joined the bulk of his party in accepting the major consequences of the Revolution, the war against France, the National Debt, and the expansion of the executive institutions of the State. The Whigs did not always wholeheartedly welcome these developments, but they were prepared to countenance them in order to save the Revolution Settlement from the threat posed by the Jacobites and their French ally. Walpole and his Whig colleagues were ready to meet the cost of securing the Protestant succession, the balanced constitution, and freedom of worship.

Chapter 2.

When Walpole entered Parliament in 1701 the Whigs were on the defensive, the backbench Tory majority was loud in its denunciation of the political corruption and the dangerous foreign policy for which they held the Whigs responsible, and the monarch was trying desperately to govern without being the prisoner of either party. This situation was to be repeated many times over the next fourteen years until the Hanoverian succession saw the final defeat of the Tory party and the dependence of the new King on Whig support. At the beginning of Walpole's career, however, and particularly after the accession of Queen Anne in 1702, it appeared more likely that the Tories would triumph and dominate the ministry. In such a confused and dangerous situation, an ambitious young man, and one new to Parliament like Walpole, might have been expected to tread warily, yet he showed no hesitation before deciding to throw in his lot with the confirmed Whigs. He had no desire to adjust his political principles to further his immediate ambition. His decision undoubtedly reduced his chances of rising quickly to high office, but his steadfast loyalty to the Whig cause over the next fourteen years put him in a very strong position to benefit from the great opportunities created for the Whigs by the Hanoverian succession.

Walpole quickly made a name for himself defending the Whig cause against the rampant Tory majority. The short-lived parliament of 1701 was dominated by the succession problem and by the Tory attacks on the policies of William III and of his recently dismissed Whig ministers. With the death in 1700 of Princess Anne's sole surviving child, the Duke of Gloucester, and with the prospect of a new war with Louis XIV, who was ready to support the Jacobite claim to the throne, William III was anxious to secure the succession after Anne in the nearest Protestant line, the House of Hanover. The Tories, few of whom were prepared to support the Jacobite cause at this stage, were willing to accept this arrangement, embodied in the Act of Settlement, but they seized the opportunity to add several clauses to this measure. Their amendments were designed as a condemnation of the conduct of William III and as an attempt to prevent any future Hanoverian sovereign from following a similar course of action. For example, many placemen were to be excluded from the Commons after the Hanoverian succession, ministers were no longer to be able to avoid impeachment by pleading the sovereign's pardon, and no war was to be waged on behalf of any territories which did not belong to the Crown of England. These clauses enshrined the prejudices of the Country element which feared the power of the Court. This element was very strong in the Tory party and it appealed to some Whigs too, but it did not enlist Walpole's support. He was determined to support the Protestant succession, but he did not sympathize with these attempts to limit the royal prerogative in future. In the debates on another bill, which was designed to secure William III's person and government from the threat posed by the Jacobites, he vehemently inveighed against those university teachers who educated their students in the principles of divine right and hereditary succession. Later, in 1703, he tried to prevent the Tories passing a bill which would give their Jacobite friends more time to swear allegiance to Queen Anne and to come to terms with the prospect of the Hanoverian succession.

In his first years in Parliament Walpole also opposed those partisan Tory measures which were designed to punish the Whigs and reduce their political influence. Although, from 1702, the country was involved in the War of the Spanish Succession and the ministers appointed by Queen Anne were moderate Tories, the Tory majority in the Commons still spent most of its time and energy in savage attacks on the Whig leaders. They attacked the Whig ministers who had served William III and tried to reduce the political influence of the Dissenters, who were among the staunchest supporters of the Whigs. Walpole helped to protect the Whig Junto from impeachment and opposed the three successive Occasional Conformity Bills which were aimed at the Dissenters. These bills sought to prevent the practice of occasional communion in the Church of England by which Dissenters endeavoured to evade the religious tests imposed on all office holders by the terms of the Test and Corporation Acts. The first two bills reached the Lords before they were defeated, but Walpole was in the vanguard of the majority which threw the third bill out of the Commons in November 1704. The intransigence of the extreme Tories lost them the support of the moderates in the party, alienated the Government, and played into the hands of the Whigs. While this was happening Walpole was rising to prominence in the Commons and was gaining favour with the Whig leaders. He was befriended by the Junto peers, was welcomed into the Kit Cat Club, and was on very close terms with all the other leading young Whig spokesmen in the Commons. Whenever important debates were pending he was always urged to lend his weight to the Whig cause. His activities on behalf of his native county when its affairs were discussed in the Commons had also strengthened his base in Norfolk. In the general election of 1702 he was so confident of his interest in Castle Rising that he was able to bring in two friends there while he shifted his seat to King's Lynn, which he represented for the next forty years. With his friend, Lord Townshend, he became the leader of the Norfolk Whigs in Parliament.

By 1705 Walpole had made enough of an impression in the Commons to gain some public recognition, when the Government decided it must force some of the extreme Tories out of office and make overtures to the more moderate Whigs. Ever since Queen Anne's accession in 1702, the ministry had been dominated by the triumvirate of Marlborough, Godolphin, and Harley. Though in the early years of Anne's reign all three of them were regarded as Tories, they were not strongly attached to either party. Their first concern was to find the best means of carrying on the Queen's Government and fighting the War of the Spanish Succession. They had no sympathy with the partisan views of either party, but they recognized that it was impossible to control Parliament without party support because the great majority of Members were enlisted under either the Whig or Tory banner. Throughout the reign of Anne these three courtiers, either separately or together, attempted to win the support of one or other of the parties without allowing the Government's policies to be dictated by the principles and prejudices of party men. In 1702 they had attempted to secure a parliamentary majority by an alliance with the moderate Tories, but they soon discovered that the extreme Tories dominated the party.

A majority of the backbench Tories refused to abandon their old grievances against the Whigs in order to assist the ministry by concentrating on the task of winning the war against France. Marlborough in particular was heavily committed to a major land campaign against the French, but he found that the Tories opposed this strategy, both within the ministry and in Parliament. The Whigs, on the other hand, supported this strategy and were also anxious to see the end of the Tory attacks on their past conduct in William's reign. For them, as for the triumvirate, the principal objective was the defeat of France. This would restore the balance of power in Europe and end the Pretender's hopes of a Stuart restoration. This identity of interest drove the triumvirate and the Whigs towards a political accommodation, though the former, particularly Robert Harley, were not easily persuaded to sever all links with the Tories and to put themselves at the mercy of the Whigs. The general election of 1705 reduced the number of extreme Tories in the Commons, but did not give either party a strong majority. This gave the triumvirate the opportunity of trying to govern without becoming the prisoner of either the Whigs or the Tories. When they decided to remodel the ministry they offered only a few minor rewards to the Whigs. Among those brought into the Government was Robert Walpole, who became one of the members of Prince George's Admiralty Council in June, 1705.

Although this was a minor appointment it certainly promoted Walpole's political career. It increased his personal influence so that he was able to assist his friends and relatives. He indulged in some profitable smuggling and allowed his friends to share in the illicit proceeds. He kept his constituency informed about admiralty decisions, particularly its arrangements to convoy merchant ships to and from the ports of East Anglia, and he obtained places for his two younger brothers. Galfridus Walpole was given a naval commission and Horatio went on the military expedition to Spain as secretary to Brigadier-General James Stanhope. His new post also brought Walpole into the centre of public affairs and to the full notice of the country's leading statesmen. It gave him the opportunity to impress them with his administrative talent and his essential moderation at a time when the Government was drifting closer and closer to the Whigs. Though the Prince's council was only a subordinate body, it did have the privilege of meeting each Sunday with the cabinet ministers in the Queen's presence to give its report on the state of the fleet. Walpole soon showed his superiors that he was the most able member of the council, for he completely mastered the intricate problems of naval supply and finance. Marlborough and Godolphin were even more satisfied at the way Walpole put the claims of the Government before the rancour of party prejudice. His political skill was of greater advantage to the ministry in the Commons than his administrative ability on the council board.

The ministry needed all the support it could get, for neither the Whigs nor the Tories were satisfied with its political complexion. Both parties continued to put pressure on the Government to force it to make concessions to their partisan demands. Walpole, although he never broke completely with the Junto Whigs, sympathized with the predicament of Marlborough, Godolphin, and Harley. His support for their efforts to win the war, which he believed must be the first priority for the Whigs, overrode his commitment to the idea of a Whig administration.

He recognized the difficulty of creating a Whig ministry when this was so strenuously opposed by the Queen. He feared, therefore, that the Junto Whigs were being too factious in their tactics of harrying the ministry, particularly during the 1707–8 parliamentary session, and so he was prepared to defend the Government in the Commons. From the date of his appointment to office in 1705 Walpole consistently voted with the Government. His loyalty was particularly valuable in this crucial session of 1707–8 when Whigs and Tories joined together in an unholy alliance to embarrass the ministry, not because they wished to share power between themselves, but in order to force the Government to come to terms with one or other of the parties if it desired to regain control of Parliament.

Neither party had a secure majority in the Commons, but the ministry could not survive without the support of one of them. When they both went into opposition the ministry's position was desperate. The first move was made by the Junto Whigs who, in November 1707, engineered a petition from 154 merchants attacking the Admiralty for neglecting to provide adequate convoys to safeguard merchant shipping. This attack was directed at Admiral George Churchill, Marlborough's wayward brother, who had Tory leanings and who was held responsible for the failings of the Admiralty and the Prince's council. Walpole admitted the justice of some of these charges and even considered resigning over the issue, but he responded to this particular attack by defending the ministry. His skill in political management helped to defeat the demand in the Commons for an inquiry into the conduct of naval affairs, but he could do nothing to prevent the Lords passing a blistering address against Churchill and the Admiralty in February 1708.

Despite Walpole's persistent support for the ministry, he was powerless to prevent the discontented Whigs and Tories from launching further savage attacks on the Government. His efforts were not enough to save the separate Scottish Privy Council, which the Government hoped to retain after the Union with Scotland because it was a useful source of patronage and a valuable electoral weapon. The Government's position became particularly perilous when the Opposition investigated the conduct of the military operations in Spain, where the allies had suffered a crushing defeat at the battle of Almanza. In the great debates on this subject the Opposition appeared to have proved that over 20,000 troops provided by parliamentary grants for the war in Spain had not in fact fought at Almanza. The ministry had a reasonable answer to this charge, but the rampant Opposition in both Houses of Parliament were not prepared to accept any explanation because they could see that they had the Government on the run. The chief ministers were forced to accept that their only hope of surviving in office lay in buying off either their Whig or their Tory critics. This meant offering tangible concessions in the form of places in the administration. Robert Harley hoped to bring the Tories to heel even if it meant ditching Godolphin, the Lord Treasurer. The Tories were not amenable to reason anyway, and so Marlborough and Godolphin were able to pursue the opposite policy. They forced Harley out of office and sought an accommodation with the Whigs. At least they could count upon the Whigs to support the ministry's war aims and Marlborough's military strategy.

The Government turned at first not to the Junto, although these Whig peers eventually forced their way into office, but to the more moderate Whigs who might serve them as well as Walpole had done. Walpole himself was advanced, in February 1708, to the post of Secretary at War, which had just been vacated by Henry St John, later Viscount Bolingbroke, who was a Tory friend of Robert Harley. This office was the most important of all junior appointments, particularly as the country was involved in the greatest war she had ever fought. Walpole was responsible for recruitment, billeting, the supply of clothes and equipment, military convoys, transport, the care of sick and wounded troops, and a whole complex of logistical details. Almost all aspects of the administration of the army, except pay and ordnance, were under his control. Moreover, for the first time, he was at the very heart of public affairs. He was in constant contact with other administrative bodies, such as the Ordnance Board and the Commissioners of Transport, he was frequently consulted by Marlborough, the Lord Treasurer, and the secretaries of state, and, during Marlborough's frequent absences abroad, he had direct access to the Queen herself. As in his previous post, however, his political role was vital to the Government. His chief problems were recruitment and supply, and it was his duty to pilot the recruiting bills and the army estimates through the Commons. These always aroused controversy because the supply of men and money for such a major war had become an enormous burden on the nation. There was increasing opposition both in and out of Parliament as the Government failed to crush France or force Louis XIV to accept its terms for a peace settlement. Walpole found it increasingly difficult to get his bills through the Commons, but he never wavered in his support for the Government's conduct of the war or Marlborough's method of fighting it. When the critics of the war protested at the heavy losses sustained at the battle of Malplaquet in 1709, Walpole denounced their malice and accused them of magnifying the number of casualties in order to tarnish the glory of Marlborough's great victory.

The failure of Marlborough's efforts to force France to her knees brought the ministry under severe pressure from the Tories and compelled it to rely increasingly on Whig support in order to control Parliament. The Whigs naturally expected further concessions in return for maintaining the ministry in office. Walpole was among those already in office who urged Marlborough and Godolphin to find places for the leaders of the Junto Whigs. His argument was reinforced by the Whig victory in the general election of 1708. In the election campaign the ministry had given some support to the Whigs for the first time, whereas the Tories suffered some reverses because of their internal divisions. Furthermore, the tide of public opinion temporarily favoured the Whigs. They gained credit with the electorate for securing the union with Scotland and for supporting Marlborough's military strategy, which the country hoped would lead to a speedy peace. In contrast, the Tories were seriously embarrassed by the recent abortive

Jacobite invasion launched from France by the Pretender. Thus, for the first and only time during Anne's reign, the Whigs had a majority in the Commons. This put them in a strong position to wring further concessions out of the ministry.

Walpole himself took advantage of the opportunities created by the Whig victory. He began weeding the Tories out of their places at the War Office and replacing them with his own Whig nominees. In conjunction with the other moderate Whigs in office he decided to throw in his lot once more with the Junto Whigs. This forced the ministry to come to terms with the Whig leaders. Despite her serious misgivings, the Queen gave way to this pressure and agreed to the requests of Marlborough and Godolphin to bring Sunderland, Somers, Wharton, and other Junto Whigs into the ministry. The Whig triumph, however, was short-lived. It was not consolidated until 1709, yet the ministry was overturned in 1710. The Queen was never reconciled to a Whig administration and turned increasingly to Robert Harley for advice and comfort. Harley's intrigues at Court and the growing unpopularity of the war paved the way for a powerful Tory reaction, though the Government helped to destroy itself by its own mistakes.

The passing of the General Naturalization Act of 1709, which Walpole supported, was followed by an influx of over ten thousand poor German refugees, who created an enormous financial, administrative, and social problem at a time when the country was already suffering from appalling weather, poor harvests, and high prices. The Government's failure to reach a peace settlement with France, partly because of the harsh terms offered to Louis XIV, was a bitter disappointment to the majority of the country gentlemen, who were groaning under the financial burden of the war. Finally, the Government's reaction to a sermon preached by a high-Tory, Dr Henry Sacheverell, focused this general discontent on an inflammatory political and religious question. On 5 November 1709 Sacheverell, preaching before the Lord Mayor of London at St Paul's, expressed the fears and prejudices of the Tory squires and their clerical allies.

He combined an attack on the Government for countenancing the practice of occasional conformity and the growth in the number of Dissenting academies, with a reassertion of the traditional political philosophy of the Tory party. He exhorted men to 'an absolute and unconditional obedience to the supreme power' and affirmed 'the utter illegality of resistance upon any pretence whatsoever'. The Whigs, nervous of the groundswell of public opinion towards the Tories, regarded this as an open attack, not only on the Toleration Act, but on the principles underlying the Revolution Settlement. It was impossible to ignore the challenge thrown down by Sacheverell, particularly as the Lord Mayor had seen fit to publish his sermon, but the Government blundered disastrously by deciding on a show-piece trial to impeach the offending cleric. This enabled Sacheverell to appear as a martyr for the old and venerated principles of the Church of England and the Tory party. The efforts to punish Sacheverell aroused widespread resentment and played straight into the hands of Robert Harley, who was seeking an excuse to bring down the ministry.

It was soon clear to both parties that their fortunes and the fate of the ministry hinged on the outcome of this trial. Walpole responded to this challenge by helping his Whig colleagues in the Commons to draft the articles of impeachment, and he himself was chosen as one of the managers who were instructed to present the prosecution's case before the Lords. In his brief, Walpole concentrated on the political aspects of the charge and presented a classic statement of Whig principles. Although he avoided exaggeration and excess, he put forward a coherent, powerful defence of the Revolution Settlement. While careful not to encourage resistance to authority on any light pretext, he denounced the doctrine of unconditional obedience and affirmed the legitimacy of overthrowing those who would abuse their power by seeking to subvert the constitutional rights of the subject. It was idle for Sacheverell and the Tories to deny that resistance had been necessary in 1688 or to claim that force had not in fact been used because of the voluntary abdication of James II. The Revolution Settlement rested squarely on Whig

principles, Walpole maintained, and Sacheverell must be prevented from preaching dangerous political doctrines, which en-
dangered the Protestant succession and promoted the cause of
the Pretender.

Sacheverell's defence tended to evade this challenge, thus
reflecting the Tory dilemma about coming to terms with the
Revolution Settlement, but the trial was not decided by the skill
of the contending counsels or the merits of the actual sermon.
The impeachment had become an emotion-charged case of defending the principles and prejudices of the two parties. The
London mob and a great deal of opinion throughout the country cared little for the logic and force of Walpole's arguments,
but clearly resented an attack upon a high-Church divine.
Courtiers, placemen, and the uncommitted peers were less concerned with defending the events of 1688 than with following
the present tide of public opinion away from the Whigs and
towards the strongest influence at Court, Robert Harley. The
result of the Sacheverell trial showed that the Whig ministry
had overreached itself. Sacheverell was found guilty, but only
by a narrow majority, and he received a very light sentence
which prevented him from preaching in public for the next
three years. Walpole feared that this was as good as acquitting
him, and his opinion was shared by the Tories, who rejoiced at
this verdict.

With the Queen's influence and public opinion clearly behind him, Robert Harley set about destroying the Godolphin
administration in the summer of 1710. Walpole hoped that Marlborough, who was indispensable if the war were to continue,
might yet save the ministry, and so he urged him to try to
remain on good terms with the Queen. He was alarmed at the
way Marlborough's control of army commissions was being
threatened so that the Queen could promote Colonel Hill, the
brother of her new favourite, Abigail Masham, but he persuaded the Captain-General that it would be disastrous for the
ministry if he resigned over this issue. He was even compelled
to see his own authority as Secretary at War challenged by one
of the Tory generals, the Duke of Ormonde, who refused to con-

sult him about the movements of his troops. Walpole believed that minor irritations and insults must be suffered in order to preserve a Whig administration. Although the ministry was clearly in the utmost danger, he hoped it might stave off defeat by presenting a united front and perhaps, in the last resort, by threatening mass resignations, including that of Marlborough. In the event the ministry failed to hold together, and Harley replaced his chief opponents one by one. His piecemeal reconstruction of the ministry culminated in the dismissal of Godolphin, though for the present Harley decided to retain the services of Marlborough.

Walpole realized that his own position was now precarious, but he still hoped that he might come to terms with Harley, who was anxious not to become the prisoner of the extreme Tories. Although he remained a loyal Whig, Walpole relished the power attached to his position as Secretary at War and was reluctant to give up the financial rewards of this office and his additional post as Treasurer of the Navy, which he had been given in January 1710. This second appointment had relieved his desperate financial plight, which was due to his notorious extravagance. It also enabled him to extricate himself a little from his close dependence on Marlborough, who dominated all matters concerned with the army. He hoped that his relative independence of Marlborough and Godolphin, his undoubted political abilities, and his moderate behaviour might yet commend him to Harley. The new head of the Treasury had no desire to see his Government packed with Tories, and so he too was ready to countenance moderate Whigs in his administration. By the end of September 1710, however, Walpole was convinced that the new ministry would be dominated by the Tories and that the forthcoming general election would result in heavy losses for the Whigs. With evident reluctance, and even in some despair, he agreed to resign his position as Secretary at War. For the time being, however, he remained Treasurer of the Navy. He had clearly established his Whig credentials and had no wish to be deprived of the income from this office. Harley may have deliberately kept him in this post in an effort to keep him from going into outright opposition to the new administration.

Harley soon showed that, despite his superb political management, he could not prevent the huge Tory majority returned
to the Commons by the 1710 general election from attacking the
conduct of the previous Whig administration. Their conduct
forced the Whigs to unite in adversity. Although they suffered
heavy losses in the general election, when Walpole himself
saw his support in Norfolk seriously reduced, the Whigs were
determined to resist Harley's plan to negotiate a speedy peace
with France. They were even more alarmed about the Hanoverian succession, which they feared might be jeopardized by the
Jacobite sympathizers among the Tory backbenchers. Throughout the last four years of Anne's reign, when they were forced
onto the defensive, the Whigs were sustained by their conviction that they must at all costs safeguard the Revolution Settlement and by their hope that the Hanoverian succession would
restore their political fortunes. Their eventual triumph owed
much to the coherence of their political philosophy and the
strength of their party organization, but they were also assisted
by the divisions among their opponents. Harley's leadership was
soon challenged by Henry St John, who was created Viscount
Bolingbroke in 1712, and Harley's moderation was rejected by
the Tory backbenchers. Moreover, it soon became apparent that
neither the ministry nor the Tory party was united on the
crucial question of who should succeed Queen Anne.

When the rebellious attitude of the Tory majority compelled Harley to placate them by dismissing all the Whigs still
holding minor office, Walpole was one of those to suffer. In
January 1711 he finally lost his post as Treasurer of the Navy.
As soon as he was released from any need to ingratiate himself
with Harley, Walpole distinguished himself as one of the most
formidable opponents of the ministry. When Harley, who had
just been created Earl of Oxford, set up the South Sea Company
as a counterpoise to the Whig moneyed corporations, Walpole
co-ordinated the opposition to his bill. Though he was unable to
defeat this measure, which was so popular with the Tories, his
efforts did win him many friends in the City. The support of the

moneyed interest was to be vital to his political success in the future. Walpole also proved his loyalty to his Whig colleagues when the Tory Commissioners of Accounts accused the previous administration of misappropriating no less than £35 million of public money voted by Parliament. These charges, which grossly exaggerated the financial corruption and mismanagement in the last Government, were directed at Marlborough, James Brydges, the paymaster of the forces abroad, and, to a lesser extent, Robert Walpole himself. Even the most prejudiced of Tories could find no evidence to convict Godolphin of mal-practices at the Treasury. Before these charges could ever be substantiated, Walpole tried to defend himself. He helped Arthur Maynwaring to write two pamphlets, *The Debts of the Nation Considered* and *A State of the Five and Thirty Millions*, in which they accused the Tories of deliberately and maliciously creating an atmosphere in which the Whigs would be con-demned for corrupt practices, when all that was amiss was the slowness of the Exchequer in passing the accounts submitted to it by the previous ministry. Although this was true, it was not a complete answer to the charge of massive corruption. The Tories were certainly not convinced by these arguments, but Oxford was able to prevent them attacking Marlborough and his friends until he was convinced that the war with France was over.

Walpole was even more active in the Commons in leading the opposition to the evident readiness of the Government to desert the allies and negotiate a separate peace with France. As early as January 1711, when the debate on the conduct of the war in Spain was renewed, Walpole expressed the fear that the ministry might exploit the military reverses in Spain in order to abandon the war altogether, without consulting the country's Dutch, Austrian, and Hanoverian allies. When, in September 1711, the ministry published the preliminary peace terms, which made it clear that the Government was prepared to accept a Bourbon king in Spain and was ready to sacrifice the interests of the allies, Walpole and his Whig colleagues were aghast. They feared that this betrayal was but the prelude to an attempt to

restore the Pretender. The Whig Opposition therefore consulted the Elector of Hanover and concerted action with the
Dutch and Austrians before launching a massive propaganda
campaign against the terms negotiated by the ministry. Walpole and the leaders of the Junto Whigs met together at Chippenham in November to discuss their tactics in the next
parliamentary session. They were greatly encouraged by the
defection of the Earl of Nottingham, the first of the pro-
Hanoverian Tories to rebel against the policies of the ministry.
Nottingham's assistance was not lightly gained, for the Whigs
were forced to agree to abandon their opposition to a new
Occasional Conformity Bill which he introduced. The Whigs
were prepared to abandon their usual policy of protecting the
interests of the Dissenters in an effort to safeguard the Hanoverian succession, their first objective. With Nottingham's support,
the Whigs in the Lords were able to pass a motion of 'no peace
without Spain' on 7 December 1711. On the same day Walpole
proposed an identical motion in the Commons, but, despite the
assistance of a few Hanoverian Tories, it was heavily defeated
by the ministry's Tory supporters.

Oxford, though shaken by his defeat in the Lords, soon
repaired his majority there by persuading the Queen to create
twelve new Tory peers. Determined to press on with the peace
negotiations, he decided to take the offensive against his Whig
opponents. Marlborough was at last dismissed from all his
posts. General Cadogan, the Duke of Somerset, and other
Whigs in office suffered a similar fate. The ministry also decided to make use of the accusations made by the Tory Commissioners of Accounts to arraign both Marlborough and
Walpole on charges of corruption in connection with contracts
for supplying the army with food and equipment. Walpole was
the first to be censured when, on 17 January 1712, he was
accused of reserving a share in the forage contract for the army
in Scotland for the personal benefit of his friend, Robert Mann.
Rather than share their profits with Mann, the contractors had
agreed to pay him 500 guineas to stay out of the agreement.
This had been done on two contracts. Due to some oversight

the bill for one payment had been made out to 'Robert Walpole or Order', though it was clear that the money had in fact gone to Mann. The prosecution could find no evidence, and none has come to light since, to prove that Walpole himself took the bribes or pocketed a percentage of army contracts. The Commons did not even know that Mann was Walpole's banker and confidential agent, which would have explained why Walpole had been so willing to oblige him by giving him a cut of these forage contracts. The partisan Tories, however, were not very much concerned with evidence, nor were they abashed by the small sums involved in the offence which they could prove against Walpole. Their sole concern was to destroy one of the leading Whig spokesmen in the Commons and a staunch critic of the peace negotiations, however flimsy the charge. They were not satisfied with merely besmirching Walpole's reputation, for they voted to expel him from the Commons and to imprison him in the Tower until the end of the parliamentary session in July 1712. The sentence kept Walpole out of the Commons while the Government completed its peace negotiations with France, but it enhanced Walpole's reputation among the Whigs by making him a martyr for the party's cause.

The Whig cause, however, seemed at a low ebb. Marlborough was censured and went into voluntary exile abroad. The allies were brow-beaten into coming into the peace negotiations or were forced to fight on without Britain's support. The peace terms negotiated at Utrecht in 1713 proved very popular with many sections of the community. Finally, the general election of 1713 gave the Tory party its greatest victory since the Revolution and reduced the Whig Opposition in the Commons to a bare 150 seats. Yet, paradoxically, these achievements only increased the tensions within the Tory party. Oxford's tortuous and secretive approach to both politics and diplomacy exasperated the impatient Tory backbenchers and provoked Bolingbroke into challenging for the leadership of the party and the Government. The Tories were divided over measures as well as men. The ministry and the party were still not united in their stand on the succession to the ailing Queen

Anne. By splitting into Jacobites, Hanoverians, and those who sat obstinately on the fence, the Tories played into the hands of the Whig minority.

Walpole and his Whig colleagues knew that they could not defeat the Tories in Parliament, but they fought a determined campaign to highlight the divisions among their opponents and to emphasize their own complete loyalty to the Hanoverian succession. They continued to oppose the peace negotiations long after it was hopeless to prevent a settlement, simply in order to convince the Elector of Hanover that the ministry could not be trusted to protect Hanoverian interests, particularly on the succession issue. Walpole was unable to speak against the Treaty of Utrecht in the Commons, because of his expulsion from the chamber, but he took up his pen to criticize it in a trenchant pamphlet, *A Short History of Parliament* (1713). In this work he not only defended himself and the previous administration against the charges of corruption levelled by the Tories, but denounced the peace settlement for not ensuring the balance of power in Europe and congratulated Parliament for rejecting the proposed commercial treaty with France. When Walpole campaigned to return to the Commons in the general election of 1713, he addressed a short manifesto to the voters of King's Lynn, telling them that the peace threatened the nation's future prosperity and hinting broadly that the present ministry was a threat to the Hanoverian succession. Such arguments may have helped him to win King's Lynn, but his Whig allies suffered reverses in the rest of Norfolk and throughout the whole country. This set-back only encouraged the Whigs to make greater efforts when Parliament met so that they could widen the evident divisions within both the ministry and the Tory party.

The obvious deterioration in the Queen's health in 1713–14 persuaded the Whigs that they would not have long to wait before their loyalty to the Hanoverian family would be rewarded. The prospect of her imminent death also drove Bolingbroke to desperate measures to overthrow Oxford and to unite the Tory party behind him. He could not give a clear lead on the succession issue, but he hoped to rally the Tory back-benchers by pursuing policies which would appeal to their pre-judices. His frantic efforts enabled him to inflict some defeats on the Whigs, but his ultimate failure allowed the Whig minor-ity to enjoy the spectacle of the ministry and the Tory party rending themselves apart. Bolingbroke rooted out those Whigs still in any position of power, particularly those with commis-sions in the army, so that they could offer no serious resistance if the Tories decided to restore the Pretender. He also helped to engineer a parliamentary attack on Richard Steele, the Whig pamphleteer, who had criticized the peace settlement in the *Importance of Dunkirk Considered* and had warned of the dan-ger of a Jacobite restoration in *The Crisis*. Walpole and James Stanhope managed Steele's defence in the debate in the Com-mons on 18 March 1714. The former protested that all Steele's accusations were justified and that only those anxious to please Louis XIV and ready to serve the Pretender could resent what Steele had written. The ministers were afraid, claimed Wal-pole, to prosecute Steele in a court of law and so resorted to their majority in the Commons to silence an honest man. Steele was being persecuted for proclaiming his loyalty to the Hano-verian succession. Thus, Walpole skilfully ignored Steele's re-marks about the peace in order to concentrate his attack on the ministry's uncertain stand on the succession issue. Walpole could not save Steele from expulsion from the Commons, but, in any case, he was less interested in the votes cast on this par-ticular occasion than in dividing the Tories, appealing to public opinion outside Parliament, and ingratiating himself with the Elector of Hanover.

In the debate on Steele's pamphlets a small number of Hanoverian Tories defected to the Whig Opposition. As the Whigs shrewdly concentrated on the alleged threat to the Pro-testant succession throughout the rest of this parliamentary session, an increasing number of Tories lost confidence in their leaders. The rebellion of Hanoverian Tories grew, while the Jacobites despaired of ever committing the Government to the restoration of the Pretender. A number of Tories, led by the Earl

of Anglesey in the Lords and Sir Thomas Hanmer in the Commons, joined the Whigs in protesting that they believed the
Hanoverian succession was in danger under the present administration. Walpole led for the Opposition in the Commons. His
speech was much acclaimed, though he could not prevent the
ministry securing a majority for a motion claiming that the
Hanoverian succession was in no danger under the present
administration. He did, however, succeed in reducing the Government's majority to less than fifty.

Bolingbroke retaliated by launching an attack on the Dissenting academies in the hope that this would bring Hanmer
and the other Hanoverian Tories back into line. Walpole spoke
up strongly for the cause of religious toleration and helped to
lead the opposition in the Commons, though he could not defeat this Schism Bill. The Whig peers also failed to reject it,
but they carried so many amendments that they virtually
emasculated it. Bolingbroke's parliamentary triumph was hard-
won and short-lived. He was unable to prevent both chambers
combining to pass measures designed to safeguard the Hanoverian succession. In the Commons a motion was passed to put
a price of £100,000 on the Pretender's head, while in the Lords
the peers moved that it should be high treason for anyone to
enlist soldiers in the Pretender's service. Bolingbroke had lost
control to such an extent that he had to urge the Queen to pro-
rogue Parliament on 9 July 1714, before the Lords made damaging disclosures about his own involvement in the shady financial
deals of the new South Sea Company. His success at Court, however, was similarly short-lived. He at last engineered the dismissal of Oxford on 27 July, but, to his everlasting regret, the
Queen fell mortally ill within hours of removing the Lord
Treasurer.

It was too late now for Bolingbroke to unite the Tories on
the succession issue. He clearly lost his nerve and took the
extraordinary step of trying to arrange a deal with the young
Whig leaders in the Commons, hoping to appeal to their political ambitions over the heads of the Junto lords, who could
expect to be the principal beneficiaries of the Hanoverian suc-

cession. Walpole was in Norfolk, or he would have been present at this bizarre encounter. James Stanhope, William Pulteney, and James Craggs did meet Bolingbroke and warned him in no uncertain terms to declare for the Elector of Hanover or face the serious consequences. Bolingbroke was crushed by their uncompromising attitude and he was in no position to give the bewildered Tories a clear lead. While the Tories hesitated, the Whigs acted. By seizing the initiative in the Privy Council and the Council of Regency, and by showing a willingness to fight if necessary, the Whig leaders ensured the peaceful accession of George I when Queen Anne died on 1 August 1714. After four years in the political wilderness the superior discipline of the Whig party and the greater coherence of its political philosophy triumphed over the numerically stronger Tories. Walpole had played a conspicuous part in this victory and he could look forward to a handsome reward when George I arrived from Hanover.

3   The Hanoverian Succession

Although the accession of George I marks the beginning of the long years of Whig supremacy and, in a sense, of one-party government in Britain, this development was by no means inevitable, and its full significance was not appreciated by the politicians of either party for some years. The Tories did not simply disappear from the political scene when Queen Anne died, nor did the Whigs maintain their discipline and unity of purpose after they had achieved their primary aim, the Hanoverian succession. Moreover, George I, with his own political views and with the advice of his German ministers, had no desire to alienate all the Tories or to become the prisoner of the Whigs. The political scene after the Hanoverian succession was almost as complicated as in the years immediately following the Revolution Settlement, though this time the Whigs adjusted to the new circumstances more quickly and exploited their advantages more successfully. Robert Walpole was rewarded with office soon after George I's accession, but he did not achieve political supremacy until he too had learned to adjust to a new era in British politics.

The death of Queen Anne destroyed the Tory Government, but it did not lead to the immediate extinction of the Tory party. The new King was reluctant to proscribe loyal Hanoverian Tories, such as Nottingham, and the Tories, despite their defeat in the general election of 1715, won more seats than the Whigs had done in 1713. If they had been united, disciplined, and well led, they might have staged a political recovery after a few years in opposition. The party, however, began to disintegrate, and within a relatively short time it had become clear that it would never again hold power. Some of its principles and prejudices survived in the hearts of backbench squires, but they did not expect to lead a Tory administration. The Tory party was demoralized and divided by the time Queen Anne died, and no outstanding leader came forward to pull it together so that it could adjust, however painfully, to the consequences of the Hanoverian Succession. Their established leaders, Oxford and Bolingbroke, were impeached for treason in 1715. Though the Whigs never found conclusive proof of their guilt, Bolingbroke's flight to France and the abortive Jacobite rebellion of 1715 were sufficient to damn the Tories in the eyes of George I. Few Tories actually took part in this rebellion, but enough of them did for the Whigs to charge all of them with disloyalty towards the Hanoverian Settlement. The Whigs soon purged the Tories from public office. They also reduced their ability to appeal to the electorate by passing the Septennial Act in 1716, which extended the maximum life of a parliament from three to seven years. This measure prevented the Tories from exploiting the disputes which broke out among the Whig leaders in 1717 and the public hostility which was expressed against the Whigs after the bursting of the South Sea Bubble in 1720. By making elections less frequent, this Act raised the value of a seat, thus giving an advantage to rich men and those attached to the Government, and made it more difficult to stampede the electorate. When the next general election was held in 1722 the Whigs were firmly entrenched in power, while the Tories had ceased to offer a viable, alternative government.

Individual Tories, however, still remained on the political scene throughout Walpole's long career in office. In fact, it is possible to identify nearly 150 Tories in the Commons even after the general election of 1741, but, as each year passed, their political significance declined. There were still a few Tories, led by William Shippen, who never came to terms with the Hanoverian succession and who remained nostalgically attached to the principles of divine right and hereditary succession. There was a much larger body of Hanoverian Tories, but they could never unite behind one leader and found it increasingly difficult to discover any distinctive Tory issue on which to oppose the

Whig administrations. Walpole and the other Whig leaders judiciously defused two emotive Tory issues by reducing the financial burden, in the shape of the land tax, on the squires and by refusing to countenance any serious attack on the privileges of the Church of England. Unable to stage many parliamentary battles on these traditional issues, the Tories had to be content with the negative criticisms and obstructive tactics of natural backbenchers. Without a positive political programme, they became a permanent element in the opposition to Walpole and the Whig supremacy. Acting as a kind of watchdog on the activities of the Government, they spent most of their energy attacking the Whig administrations on such issues as the number of placemen in the Commons, the infrequency of general elections, the corruption in elections and public life, and the size of the standing army in peacetime. Not surprisingly, an increasing number of Tories with talent and ambition became frustrated with such a negative role. Some tried to find the basis for a more effective Opposition, but the longer Whigs like Walpole were in power, the more such able Tories deserted their traditional allegiances and defected to the Whigs. By the end of Walpole's career most Tories were backbench squires, critical of the consequences of the Whig supremacy, but with a negative, 'Country' philosophy.

Although the Whigs began a long period of political supremacy after the Hanoverian succession, they too were altered by the changing circumstances of political life. Whereas the Tories were faced with the insoluble problems created by their exclusion from political office, the Whigs had to adjust to a virtual monopoly of power. Lacking serious political rivals to keep a measure of party discipline, and with too many able and ambitious men competing for power, the leading Whigs fell prone to personal and factious struggles. This development was probably exacerbated by the fact that the old, respected Junto leaders, with the exception of Sunderland, the youngest of them, died or retired from politics soon after the Hanoverian succession. The younger generation of Whig spokesmen, notably Walpole, Stanhope, Townshend, and Pulteney, were soon scrambling for the leading positions. They tended to gather around them groups or factions of politicians and friends who hoped to join them in office. The political arena no longer saw a clash of Whig and Tory parties, but a battle among groups of Whigs about who should be in and who should be left out of power. While the 'ins' looked to their Whig allies and to the Court for support, the 'outs' usually sought a temporary alliance with the Tory or independent backbenchers in order to force their way into office. These usually proved to be alliances of convenience rather than of principle.

As a consequence of these developments the Whig party gradually lost some of its cohesion and some of its distinctive features. The leading Whigs in office, particularly Robert Walpole, were able to retain the loyalty of a considerable body of Whigs, which came to be known as the Old Corps, because they skilfully exaggerated and exploited the threat to the Hanoverian succession. In addition to the fears created by Jacobite rebellions and conspiracies, the strong personality of Walpole and the shrewd dispensation of patronage helped to hold this body of Whigs together. Nevertheless, during Walpole's long administration from 1721 to 1742, there were not many other vestiges of Whig principles attaching to the Government or its principal supporters. Walpole accepted the basis of the Treaty of Utrecht, which had been negotiated by his Tory enemies, and pursued a policy of friendship with France and the careful avoidance of a major European war. In debates on the constitution Walpole and the other leading Whigs were less ready to assert the rights of Parliament against the royal prerogative. Now that the royal prerogative and the Crown's patronage could be used by Whig administrations, Whig ministers were less anxious to see these powers reduced. Some radical Whigs on the backbenches still demanded further reductions of the Crown's influence, more frequent and less corrupt general elections, and greater individual liberty, but these objectives were no longer so attractive to those Whigs who achieved high office. The Whig administrations became more conservative under the early Hanoverians and real political power was restricted to a narrow oligarchy of large land-owners, wealthy financiers, and great merchants. These men, having preserved the Protestant succession and the balance of power between Crown and Parliament, and having reaped such rich personal rewards, were increasingly content to enjoy the fruits of power and office. The long years of the Whig supremacy, particularly the two decades when Walpole dominated the administration, saw the leading Whigs become complacent and somewhat neglectful of their original Revolution principles, though they never entirely retreated from the achievements of the Revolution Settlement.

As the discipline and cohesion of the Whig and Tory parties weakened and as the political and constitutional distinctions between them blurred, the structure of parliamentary politics altered. There was some resemblance to a two-party system in that governments under the first two Hanoverian monarchs always described themselves as Whig, whereas some of their staunchest critics survived from the remnants of the Tory party of Anne's reign. The narrow struggle for ministerial power, however, was fought out between groups or factions, the 'ins' and 'outs', which were rarely divided on questions of principle. The broader struggle for dominance in Parliament was largely a contest between the friends of the ministry, 'the Court', and their opponents, who are usually referred to as 'the Country'. The Court could generally count upon the support of the ministerial group, those members holding offices, places, and pensions under the Crown, and the staunch Whigs of the Old Corps. The Country Opposition was an uneasy alliance of Whig 'outs' and the remnants of the Tory party. Together, however, the Court and the Country only made up between a half and two-thirds of the House of Commons. There was a vital third element, the independent backbenchers. These Members were usually country gentlemen of independent means and independent attitudes. They did not hold office under the Crown and had no desire to do so, but neither did they believe in permanent, factious opposition to the Court. They were not committed to either the Court or the Country, but they were prepared to be swayed by the arguments and actions of either. Since they held the balance of power in the Commons, the success of the ministry or the Opposition depended on their ability to win over these independent Members. Ministries could not long survive when they lost the confidence of these country gentlemen on the backbenches.

The Hanoverian succession did not only affect the fortunes and nature of the Whig and Tory parties and the basic structure of parliamentary politics. It also introduced new features into the political life of the nation. George I never became the mere instrument of the Whigs and, particularly in his first years on the throne, he relied heavily on his German advisers. Both the first two Hanoverian monarchs were more sympathetic to Hanoverian interests than to those of their new kingdom. They both strove to spend every summer in Hanover and they both laboured to defend Hanover from any enemy on the Continent, even if this meant using British resources to achieve this end. As a result the leading Whigs had to learn how to pander to these German prejudices and how to persuade Parliament to vote the necessary men and supplies, which might be needed to defend the Electorate of Hanover. Parliament, however, was not always prepared to accept the Government's arguments that it was not sacrificing British interests.

In addition, the ministers faced another new political embarrassment; this one created by the reversionary interest. Throughout Walpole's career under the early Hanoverians he had to tackle the delicate political problem of how to handle the heir to the throne. Both George I and George II had to reckon with the personal hostility and political opposition of their eldest sons. Both kings tried to prevent their heirs having any independent political power, but they could not deny them all political influence. The Prince of Wales had some patronage at his disposal which helped him to attract some politicians to his cause, while other ambitious politicians, who were out of office, supported him to further their own careers. They could proclaim their loyalty to the Hanoverian Settlement and purge themselves of any taint of Jacobitism, while bitterly attacking the Whig administrations of the day.

Robert Walpole, despite the reputation which he had earned among the Whigs in the last years of Anne's reign, was still not in a position to push himself to the summit of political power on the accession of George I. Townshend, who had recently married Walpole's favourite sister, Dorothy, was appointed one of the new secretaries of state, but Walpole only became Paymaster-General. This post did not give him much influence when the Government discussed policy, but it did have its compensations. Even in peacetime it was the most lucrative of all government posts. The Paymaster received large sums of money from the Treasury every year. There was nothing to prevent him investing this money and pocketing the interest before he was called upon to disburse these funds among the troops. Walpole seized this opportunity to enrich himself in order to support the extravagant life he loved so much. The Paymastership also controlled a great deal of patronage, which Walpole exploited to help his relatives and friends at the expense of minor Tory officials. Moreover, it also provided Walpole with the quiet retreat at Chelsea that he retained for the rest of his political life. He used it when he could not spare the time to escape further afield to Houghton, the family seat in Norfolk.

For the first time Walpole began to grow rich and was able to indulge in the lavish hospitality and opulent display for which he became increasingly famous or notorious, but he was never solely interested in money. Political power was always his first aim and his real love. Wealth was an exciting by-product of power and, indeed, a public symbol of it, and Walpole had no scruples about amassing a fortune by dubious, if not blatantly corrupt, methods; but he was more interested in controlling government policy and dominating other men. The position of Paymaster-General did not satisfy his political ambitions and so he strove to increase his stature in Parliament and among the Whig majority. He campaigned vigorously in the general election of 1715 in order to secure the kind of Whig majority needed to safeguard the Hanoverian succession and to crush the Tory party. Walpole was not content to let the Tories gradually come to terms with the new dynasty and perhaps compete again with the Whigs for political power. He wanted to destroy completely what limited credit they still retained with the new King and yet also prevent them becoming a troublesome Opposition. His task was made easier by the evident sympathy of some of the Tories for a Jacobite restoration.

In the royal proclamation for a general election in 1715, which Walpole helped to draft, he inserted a reference to the danger which had threatened the Hanoverian succession in the last years of Anne's reign. When the new parliament met, Walpole moved the Royal Address, which he had probably composed with Stanhope, condemning the previous Tory administration. This was a declaration of war on the Tories, and the ensuing debate made it clear that the Tories did not have the numerical strength to defend their leaders. Anticipating impeachment and fearing for his head, Bolingbroke lost his nerve and, early in April 1715, he fled to France. His flight played into the hands of Walpole and the Whigs, who claimed that this was a clear demonstration of guilt. Conclusive evidence for the charges of Jacobitism that Walpole had so frequently levelled at the previous Tory ministers was never in fact produced, but Bolingbroke's flight, the pro-Jacobite disturbances in many parts of England, and then the 1715 rebellion, condemned the Tory party. Not only those Tories directly involved in these events, but the whole party, both retrospectively and forever, was smeared with the taint of disloyalty to the Hanoverian succession. Walpole took full advantage of this opportunity provided by his political enemies. He was chosen as chairman of the Committee of Secrecy which was set up to investigate the activities of the recent Tory Government. With unflagging determination and implacable hostility he sifted a mass of evidence to produce a lengthy, if not entirely conclusive, indictment of the previous administration. On 9 June 1715 it took Walpole five hours to read to the Commons all the charges against Bolingbroke, Oxford, Ormonde, and Strafford. The political careers of these Tory leaders were effectively destroyed, even though the case against them was never proved. Oxford was eventually acquitted, but Bolingbroke and Ormonde were condemned by Acts of Attainder because they chose to serve the Pretender during the 1715 rebellion.

This Jacobite rebellion frightened the Whig Government even though it was quickly put down. Walpole, who had been rewarded for his recent services by being promoted First Lord of the Treasury and Chancellor of the Exchequer, was determined that the defeated rebels should be shown no mercy. When faced with the Jacobite menace he abandoned all his habitual moderation. Always fearful, to an almost pathological extent, for the security of the Hanoverian Settlement, he was prepared to pursue any Jacobite to the grave. Despite his vigorous efforts in the Commons, however, only two rebels were in fact executed, though he and his Whig colleagues were able to purge the administration of the few Tories still holding minor places. Even Nottingham, a Hanoverian Tory, was forced out of office for advocating that the ministry should pursue a policy of clemency towards the rebels. Though they destroyed their main Tory opponents and extended the life of their parliamentary majority by passing the Septennial Act in 1716, the Whig leaders soon fell out among themselves. The enticing prospect of monopolizing political power increased the inevitable tensions of too many able men chasing too few posts of real influence and power. By mid-1716 the small world of the Whig oligarchy was riven by factional strife as the younger generation fought for supreme power once the Whig Junto had left the political scene.

Sunderland, who had been made Lord Lieutenant of Ireland and then Lord Privy Seal by George I, was jealous of the more important offices held by the less-experienced Townshend and Walpole. He soon made common cause with Stanhope, who genuinely disagreed with Townshend, Stanhope's fellow-Secretary of State, over the conduct of foreign affairs. Townshend was less concerned than Stanhope about the fate of Hanover and about the consequences for that electorate of the great war being waged by all the major Baltic powers. George I was most anxious for an alliance with France so that the royal navy would be free to intervene more effectively in the Baltic and so safeguard Hanover's interests in the region. Townshend's attitude weakened his influence with the King and his German ministers and mistresses, while Walpole, too, was soon being criticized for not providing the necessary funds to pay the German mercenaries hired by the King. At the same time, and as an additional complication, the Prince of Wales, who resented his lack of political influence even when he acted as regent during his father's annual visits to Hanover, had begun to conspire with such discontented Whigs as the Duke of Argyll in order to embarrass the ministry. Sunderland claimed that Walpole and Townshend were deliberately fomenting the opposition of the Prince of Wales. Stanhope, who was uncertain of his authority within the ministry and who disagreed with the foreign policy advocated by Walpole and Townshend, began to take Sunderland's claims seriously. Despite the friendly letters which were exchanged between the two sides, the rift widened throughout 1716. Walpole, preoccupied with the size of the National Debt and fearful of the consequences of an active policy in the Baltic, was most concerned about the potential opposition in Parliament to the ministry's conduct. Stanhope, in Hanover with the King, focused on the European situation and the need to satisfy George I's demands to protect Hanoverian interests. Though Sunderland did everything to widen the breach, Stanhope and Walpole were anxious to avoid an open split in the ministry. They could not reach an agreement, however, and it was soon evident that Stanhope and Sunderland were united against Walpole and Townshend. Since the root cause of the dissension was the difference of opinion on foreign policy, and since Stanhope had the ear of the King on this issue, Townshend was forced to exchange his post as Secretary of State for that of Lord Lieutenant of Ireland. When he continued to criticize the ministry's policies, he was dismissed early in April 1717. Walpole resigned his posts and followed his friend into opposition. They were soon joined by their closest allies. William Pulteney, Paul Methuen, and the Duke of Devonshire resigned, while Sir Charles Turner, Sir William St Quinten, and other friends were dismissed. The rift between the leading Whigs was now complete. Walpole had lost the most important government office he had ever held. He had now to learn how best to oppose a Whig administration and how to force his way back into power without a united Whig party behind him.

Walpole's love of power made him determined to recover it as soon as possible, but power was more easily desired than gained. In opposition his position was far from strong. Despite the suggestions which were given widespread currency later, there is no reliable evidence that George I hated losing his services or desired his rapid return to office. Nor did the Prince and Princess of Wales welcome him with open arms. Moreover, even if he were to curry favour with them, this would only alienate the King and make it more difficult to return to power. Although he had some able Whig supporters, the bulk of the party remained loyal to the Stanhope–Sunderland administration. Walpole might snipe at the Government's policies for years before he found an issue which would bring about massive Whig defections to the Opposition and destroy the Government's majority. His ability in debate, his skill in parliamentary tactics, and his knowledge of public business were not enough. He needed votes to endanger the ministry's control of the Commons. Votes in sufficient numbers could only be secured from Tory backbenchers, but the pursuit of this policy was fraught with danger. Walpole would have to abandon some of his Whig principles, pander to the prejudices of the Tory squires, and risk his reputation for political integrity and consistency. Yet, even if he gained Tory votes by such an approach, he could never expect nor desire to lead the Tories into office. His only hope, therefore, was that he might be able to make such a nuisance of himself that the Whig ministers would bring him back into the ministerial fold.

Although Walpole believed that he had no alternative but to oppose the ministry, he was reluctant to turn his back on his former conduct. He had no wish to encourage a Tory revival or to endanger the Hanoverian Settlement. The grievances of the Tory squires and the unpopularity of George I were based in part on the financial legacy of the recent wars with France, namely a high level of direct taxation on land and a great increase in the size of the National Debt. In his short period as Chancellor of the Exchequer Walpole had drawn up a scheme to put the nation's finances on a firmer foundation by reducing the National Debt and thereby requiring less revenue to meet the interest costs on these loans. His plan was twofold: to consolidate much of the Debt at 5 per cent interest and to reduce the principal. New government loans were to be raised at 5 per cent interest and this money was to be used to buy up the old, redeemable stock which carried rates of interest of up to 9 per cent. A Sinking Fund was also to be established by which surplus revenue was to be used each year to redeem part of the National Debt. Stanhope, who had replaced Walpole as the head of the Treasury although he could not match his ability in this office, recognized the merits of Walpole's sound, practical scheme and proposed to introduce it himself. Walpole, to his credit, had no intention of opposing the plan, but he was enraged when Stanhope cast aspersions on his conduct when in office, charging him with seeking to enrich his relatives, his friends, and himself. He replied by accusing the King's Hanoverian advisers of seeking greater financial rewards for themselves than ever he had secured for his friends. This exchange was so bitter that many Members feared it might provoke a duel. The Speaker was asked to order the two protagonists not to let their quarrel take such a dangerous turn. A duel was avoided, but this dispute encouraged Walpole to pursue a policy of outright, even factious, opposition to the administration. This determined pursuit of power led him to compromise some of his Whig principles.

Walpole let Stanhope's financial proposals pass unopposed, but he then set about criticizing virtually every other action of the Government. In the parliamentary session of 1717 he attacked the ministry for the mismanagement and possible embezzlement of public money spent on transporting Dutch troops during the recent Jacobite rebellion. He also embarrassed the ministry by refusing to continue his earlier attempts to impeach the Earl of Oxford, who was finally acquitted by the Lords of the charges raised against him by the impeachment of 1715. Before the next session Walpole strengthened his position by reaching an accommodation with the Prince of Wales. In September 1717 the Prince quarrelled with his father because the King insisted that the Duke of Newcastle, in his capacity as Lord Chamberlain, should attend the christening of the Prince's son. Newcastle's presence was openly resented by the Prince. The terrified minister even feared that he might be challenged to a duel. Though Newcastle misunderstood the Prince's language and gestures, the King was furious at this insult to one of his principal servants. He expelled the Prince from St James's Palace and the heir to the throne set up a rival court at Leicester House. Walpole, Townshend, and other Opposition Whigs rushed to pay their respects and to secure the support of the Prince and Princess before the next parliamentary session.

The 1717–18 session revealed Walpole's capacity as an Opposition leader and showed the Government's weakness in the Commons. In December 1717 Walpole was able to rouse the backbenchers over the issue of the standing army, though he wisely made no move to have it disbanded. In view of the threat still posed by the Pretender, Walpole shrewdly concentrated on the sheer size of the army and on the imbalance between the numbers of officers and men that made this army so expensive to maintain. His penetrating criticisms and his expert handling of the financial details forced the Government to reduce its demands for money for the upkeep of the army. In the next session Stanhope antagonized the Tory squires and most of the Anglican clergy in his efforts to please the Dissenters by repealing the Occasional Conformity and Schism Acts which had been passed in Anne's reign, but he had the satisfaction of seeing Walpole betray his Whig principles. Walpole tried hard to justify his opposition to this attempt to reward the Dissenters for their political loyalty to the Hanoverian Settlement, but his speech was not convincing and he was deserted by some of his Whig allies.

Walpole's greatest success in the Commons was his defeat of Stanhope's Peerage Bill. Stanhope proposed to abolish the system of sixteen representative Scottish peers and to replace them by twenty-five hereditary peers, chosen by the Government. In addition, six new peers were to be created, but thereafter no new peers could be created except to replace a peerage which had become extinct. This scheme would strengthen the present ministry's influence in the Lords and prevent either the King's German ministers or the Opposition Whigs from being able to persuade George I to alter the new balance of forces in the upper chamber. Stanhope originally planned to introduce this measure during the 1718–19 session, but he decided to defer it until the following session. This gave Walpole the opportunity to campaign against this project even before it was laid before Parliament. In December 1719 he denounced it in two trenchant pamphlets. His opposition to it was probably genuine, but he also regarded it as providing him with an excellent opportunity of winning over the independent country gentlemen, even those who generally favoured the Government. In his attack on the bill when it appeared before the Commons he made one of the greatest speeches of his life. He protested that it would remove a valuable incentive in political life by creating a closed oligarchy, which could no longer be entered by men of ability and ambition. The bill would also disturb the balance of the constitution by making the Lords independent of both the Crown and the Commons, when the upper chamber ought to be open to the influence of both. Thus, Walpole skilfully played on the secret ambitions of even the most independent of backbenchers, who hoped to see their families ennobled, and aroused their fears of ministerial power. The hopes and fears of the backbenchers carried the day. The Peerage Bill was defeated by nearly a hundred votes on 8 December 1719. Walpole had engineered an astonishing Opposition victory.

One defeat in the Commons, however great, could not bring down a ministry which retained the King's support. George I fully approved of Stanhope's foreign policy and was determined to keep him in office. If he and his ministers had not become convinced of the wisdom of buying off Walpole and his friends, they might have weathered the political storm. The ministers had been sounding out Walpole to discover his terms ever since 1718, and the defeat of the Peerage Bill shook their confidence in managing the Commons without his support, but they finally decided to reach an accommodation only after Walpole had demonstrated his skill at court intrigue. Walpole had learned that power was shared between the Court and the Commons. He had got on good terms with the King's favourite mistress, the Duchess of Kendal, and through this channel Walpole was able to offer the King two valuable services. He promised to support in the Commons a proposal to raise £600,000 to pay the accumulated debts on the King's civil list and to persuade the Prince of Wales to submit to his father. Even though he had previously attacked the ministry for its financial extravagance, Walpole had no difficulty in helping to achieve the first part of this bargain. He simply deserted the Opposition and supported the Government's scheme, which he had helped to prepare, for raising the money to pay the King's debts. The second task, though it was accomplished on 23 April 1720, had been much harder to achieve. The King still hated his son and was determined to humiliate him. The Prince had no desire to seek a reconciliation, but was forced to submit. Walpole had come to exercise great influence on him through his able wife, Princess Caroline. Her temperament and love of power closely matched those of Walpole, and she had come to trust his political judgement. Nevertheless, the Prince was not easily persuaded to give way, and he resented Walpole's advice that he should crave the King's forgiveness for his earlier misconduct. Walpole persuaded the Prince partly by making him a fortune in South Sea Company stock, then advancing rapidly in price, and partly by warning him that he would be politically isolated if Walpole went over to the ministry before he was reconciled to his father. Prince George gave way, but he remembered the humiliation and bore Walpole a grudge for several years.

Once the debts on the civil list had been paid and the Prince had humbled himself before the King, Walpole received his reward. In June 1720 he once more became Paymaster-

General, while Townshend was appointed Lord President of the Council, and Paul Methuen was made Comptroller of the Household. The ministers were also prepared to combine with Walpole and Townshend to break the power of the Hanoverian ministers in England, but they would not offer any further concessions to the Walpole–Townshend group. William Pulteney regarded this as an act of betrayal, but Walpole was not in a position to stand out for further concessions. He himself had been forced to accept a minor office, after he had once been head of the Treasury. He was neither in the cabinet nor among the favourites at Court. The occasional success in the Commons and skilful intrigue at Court were not enough to guarantee a man, even one as able as Walpole, great political power. But for the disaster of the South Sea Bubble, which ruined the political reputations of his chief rivals and provided him with an opportunity to display his consummate political and financial skills to full advantage, Walpole might never have achieved supreme power.

4   Walpole Consolidates his Power

A proper understanding of Walpole's role after the bursting of the South Sea Bubble is vital if we are to explain why he was able to push himself to the head of the ministry so soon after returning to office in a relatively junior capacity. The traditional view, modelled on the account given in William Coxe's massive biography of Walpole that was published in 1798, was that Walpole had always opposed the South Sea Company's scheme to take over the National Debt, had forecast financial ruin when the proposal was accepted by the Government, and had been brought to the head of affairs by the widespread recognition that only he could save the country from disaster. C. B. Realey and, to a greater extent, J. H. Plumb have proved conclusively that Walpole did not foresee the spectacular crash of the speculative boom inspired by the South Sea Company and only narrowly escaped losing a fortune in the general financial collapse when the bubble burst. While this argument has been accepted, it does appear that Walpole's success in restoring the country's finances after the crash has not been given its due recognition. It needed the financial skill of Walpole and not merely the healing hand of time to restore confidence in the nation's financial system. Walpole exploited this opportunity and displayed his remarkable abilities, while some of the leading ministers in the Government were ruined. He gained favour at Court and pushed his way back to the head of the Treasury. Though he was unpopular in Parliament for some time, he was in a position to strengthen his hold on power.

The National Debt had been created in the early 1690s. The Whigs had largely created and thereafter fully supported this system of public credit because it stabilized the country's finances after the 1688 Revolution and enabled the country to fight two major wars against France. These wars, however, vastly increased the size of the National Debt and the burden of taxation needed to pay the interest on the loans. This tax burden, particularly the land tax of four shillings in the pound, was bitterly resented by most landowners, and their sense of grievance had encouraged many of them to support the Tory party, which regarded itself as the defender of the landed interest. In order to reconcile many of these country gentlemen to the Hanoverian succession, the Whigs hoped to reduce the size of the National Debt and thus the tax burden needed to pay the interest on it. This political objective had lain behind Walpole's scheme in 1717 to fix the rate of interest on the National Debt at a uniform 5 per cent and to reduce the Debt itself by means of his Sinking Fund. The same objective also persuaded Stanhope's ministry to accept the South Sea Company's proposal to take over the National Debt and reduce the financial demands on the Government to pay the interest rates.

The South Sea Company, which was becoming more of a financial than a trading corporation, planned to take over the whole National Debt, including those loans subscribed by the Bank of England and the East India Company. This grandiose scheme was strongly resisted by the Bank of England, the greatest of the Government's creditors. Walpole, who for some years had been on very intimate terms with the directors of the Bank, agreed to put the Bank's case before the Commons in January 1720. He argued with great force that the Bank had far greater experience than the South Sea Company in handling the National Debt and should be allowed even greater responsibility for raising the loans needed by the Government. Subsequent events were to prove the wisdom of Walpole's claim, but, as a result of Walpole's arguments, the ministry only agreed to except the government stock held by the Bank and the East India Company from the scheme put forward by the South Sea Company. In their proposal the company offered the Government over seven million pounds for the opportunity of being able to take over that part of the National Debt not held by the Bank and the East India Company and agreed to accept an interest rate on this stock of 5 per cent up to 1727 and of only 4 per cent thereafter. Provided the scheme actually worked, the Government and, of course, the nation would greatly benefit. In order to make it work, the South Sea Company had to persuade the holders of government stock, including irredeemable annuities which could only be surrendered voluntarily even to the Government, to exchange their stock for South Sea Company stock, which only promised an interest rate of 5 per cent. In addition, however, the company offered the enticing prospect of much greater financial rewards, though these in fact never materialized. The company had the monopoly of Britain's trade with Spanish America, trade which was expected to bring in fabulous profits. The company also hoped that, having earned the goodwill of the Government, it might in future secure the privilege of undertaking other profitable enterprises. If the company's extravagant hopes of large trading profits had been fulfilled, the scheme might have worked.

The confidence of the directors, reinforced by the Government's acceptance of the scheme, persuaded many holders of government annuities to exchange these for South Sea stock. Indeed, their frantic rush to do so pushed up the price of South Sea stock until it reached an astronomical £1,050 for £100 of stock by 24 June 1720. This boom enabled the directors of the company to engage in some sharp practices which the Government failed to prevent. The ministry had failed to ensure that the ratio of South Sea stock to be exchanged for government annuities should be clearly fixed. As the price of South Sea stock rose rapidly, so the directors were able to offer less of their stock in exchange for the annuities held by the public creditors. By June 1720, for example, they were in a position to offer £100 of South Sea stock in return for £1,000 worth of government annuities. They could then sell the £900 worth of South Sea stock which they had saved by this exchange. Their own evident success, and the profits made by those who bought South Sea stock at one price and then sold it soon afterwards when the price had soared, encouraged a wild speculative boom. All kinds of fraudulent and impractical companies, including a project to establish a chain of pawnbrokers and a scheme to prevent Englishmen being sold into slavery, were floated to take advantage of those who were eager to invest their money in the hope of reaping a quick profit but who could not afford the astronomical price of South Sea stock.

Sane men began to see the dangers of this kind of financial speculation. The Government, with the support of the South Sea Company, quickly passed the Bubble Act in 1720 to prevent such unauthorized companies being established. Unfortunately, by pricking the financial bubble, the Government damaged the South Sea Company, whose fortunes required a rising market. The price of South Sea stock suddenly slumped and, by September 1720, the company's plight had become desperate. Those holders of government annuities, who had exchanged these safe investments for South Sea stock in the hope of selling this stock on a rising market, now discovered that they had struck a bad bargain. They were left holding stock which was worth far less than their original annuities. Their rage knew no bounds when it became clear that they had suffered heavy financial losses whereas the directors of the South Sea Company and many members of the Government had made fortunes out of the recent wave of speculation on the stock market. Since many of those who had lost heavily were Members of Parliament, the plight of the ministry in the Commons was almost as desperate as that of the South Sea Company.

Robert Walpole had criticized the South Sea Company's scheme when it was first mooted in the Commons, and he had put his finger on what was to become the most dangerous aspect of the venture when he urged that the ratio of South Sea stock to be exchanged for government annuities should be clearly fixed by Parliament. His failure to carry this particular amendment, however, did not lead him to expect the financial disaster which later occurred or to stand aloof from the wave of speculation in the summer of 1720. Walpole had preferred the Bank of England's offer to take over the management of the whole

National Debt and he had criticized some of the details of the South Sea Company's proposals, but he had not attacked the fundamentals of their scheme. Not only did he secure South Sea stock at advantageous terms for the Prince and Princess of Wales, in order to curry favour at Leicester House, but he rushed to invest heavily himself. So far was he from expecting a crash that he began to buy South Sea stock for the second time when it was at its highest level in June 1720 after selling his original stock for a small profit in the previous March. As late as August 1720, when the speculative boom had passed its peak, he was still prepared to buy South Sea stock and was only saved from making substantial losses by the greater wisdom of his London banker and agent, Robert Jacombe, who advised restraint and expressed doubts about the future prospects of the South Sea Company. Walpole had made some profits from other speculative ventures, but even then he used the money to buy land in Norfolk when prices were very high. He showed no real appreciation of the danger or the magnitude of the impending disaster until the bubble burst and the stock market collapsed.

Walpole's subsequent reputation for expecting this disaster was undeserved. It was based on his earlier reservations about the venture and his good fortune in not losing heavily in the rage of speculation during the summer of 1720. Nevertheless, his contribution to the restoration of financial stability after the crash has probably been underestimated by some recent historians. In mid September 1720 Walpole used his influence with the directors of the Bank of England to persuade them to bail out the South Sea Company by offering to buy its stock at £400 for £100 of stock, but, when the market price fell well below this figure, the Bank backed out of the agreement. When he realized he could do no more for the present, Walpole wisely decided to retreat to Norfolk. He hoped to dissociate himself from the intensely unpopular ministry, but he had no desire to lead the opposition to it. This would lose him the credit at Court that he had only recently regained. It might also endanger the stability of the Whig supremacy and the Hanoverian Settlement, for the Tories and Jacobites hoped to exploit the Government's unpopularity to their advantage. Though he had no desire to salvage the reputations of the leading ministers, Walpole believed that if he could restore the nation's finances he would earn the gratitude and support of the King, the Commons, and the public. To be successful, he needed to deploy all his political and financial skill.

It was Robert Jacombe, his banker, who first suggested to Walpole that the National Debt should be divided more equally between the Bank, the South Sea Company, and the East India Company in order to reduce the crippling burden which was threatening to destroy the South Sea Company. When Walpole returned to London in November 1720, just before the Government faced an enraged Parliament, he set about putting Jacombe's proposals into effect. He contacted the directors of the Bank, who had some faith in his financial ability, and he seemed at first to have persuaded them to come into the scheme to restore public credit. The other ministers and the King had no choice but to let Walpole conduct these negotiations single-handed and to act on behalf of the whole Government.

It has been argued that these negotiations achieved nothing except to provide a breathing-space, which offered time for calmer counsels to prevail and for confidence in the essential stability of the country's economy to be restored. Thus, the country's finances ultimately repaired themselves because trade had not been disrupted and the South Sea Bubble had not destroyed wealth, but merely redistributed it on a considerable scale. This is to deny Walpole much of the credit which is his due. Under Walpole's direction the Government first made a firm stand against the demands of the enraged public creditors, who were seeking to get out of their agreement with the South Sea Company, and then devised some relief measures. Walpole's attempt to get the Bank and the East India Company to exchange £18 million of their combined stock for South Sea stock, though it was embodied in an Act of Parliament, was never put into effect. Nevertheless, Walpole did draw up a bill in the summer of 1721 that helped to restore public credit. By this scheme

Walpole forced the South Sea Company and the public creditors to abandon their extravagant and unrealistic demands. The South Sea Company was excused from paying several million pounds of the sum it had originally promised the Exchequer, but it had to disgorge all of its surplus stock. This was then shared out among the public creditors who had come into the last three subscriptions for South Sea stock in 1720. Though this gave the creditors some compensation, they were forced to stick to their bargains with the company and to reconcile themselves to drastic capital losses ranging from 25 to 50 per cent of their original holdings in government annuities. They received a little additional relief when a sum of over £2 million was confiscated from those convicted of inspiring the South Sea Company's scheme and distributed among them. Finally, in 1722, another Act allowed the Bank to buy up some of the company's annuities and at last put the company on a firm foundation. The company soon became a reliable financial corporation dealing primarily in gilt-edged government securities.

The political crisis facing the country after the bursting of the South Sea Bubble was probably more dangerous than the financial disaster. There can be no doubt that Walpole did more than anyone to solve this problem. Thousands of men with political influence had been ruined or badly hit by the financial crash. The King and his Whig ministers were more unpopular throughout the country than at any time since the Jacobite rebellion of 1715 and the Opposition in Parliament was more dangerous than at any time since the Hanoverian succession. Men who had suffered heavy financial losses were in no mood to remain quiet while Walpole and the Government strove to restore the nation's finances. They were loud and insistent in their demands for vengeance on those who had duped them into wasting their fortunes. The leading ministers were in no position to quieten their fears or ameliorate their anger, for they were all implicated in the South Sea Company's fraudulent scheme. Stanhope, Sunderland, John Aislabie, the Chancellor of the Exchequer, and the two James Craggs, father and son, had all supported the company's proposals in return for the privilege of investing heavily in South Sea stock before its price soared. Walpole's hands were relatively clean, since he had been in opposition when the scheme was approved, but even his innocence and his undoubted skill in handling the Commons could not prevent the Opposition insisting on a committee of inquiry into the whole affair.

Once this committee was appointed and was seen to be dominated by the leading critics of the Government, Walpole had to make some concessions to it if the ministry were ever to regain control of Parliament. Yet he knew it would destroy his influence at Court if he allowed the committee to condemn the King's favourite ministers and perhaps implicate the royal family itself in the fraudulent practices of the South Sea Company. The only way to save the great was to sacrifice the less influential. Aislabie, the Chancellor of the Exchequer, who was not powerful at Court, and the directors of the company were convicted of corrupt practices and much, though not all, of their wealth was confiscated. The demand for vengeance was also partially satisfied when three members of the ministry died. James Stanhope died of apoplexy while speaking in the Lords, the younger James Craggs died of smallpox, whilst his father probably committed suicide to avoid conviction and financial ruin. These events allowed Walpole to concentrate on saving Charles Stanhope and the Earl of Sunderland. The former was narrowly acquitted by three votes, but he had to resign from office. Sunderland fared better and was acquitted by a majority of more than sixty votes.

Walpole's moderation and his skilful management of the Commons saved the ministry from complete collapse in the face of a furious and vociferous Opposition. His success, limited though it was, earned him many enemies in and out of Parliament. Throughout the rest of his life he never quite lost his reputation for screening villainy and corruption, but he could congratulate himself that on this occasion his achievement had brought him to the forefront of political power. Earl Stanhope and several other potential rivals were removed from the political scene. Sunderland remained, but even he had to give up public office. In contrast, Walpole's actions and abilities secured him the recognition and even the gratitude of the King. Facing his severest test to date, he had clearly demonstrated that he had no rival as a financial minister or as a manager of the House of Commons. This combination of financial and political skill brought him to power now and kept him in office for more than twenty years. In April 1721 Walpole was again appointed Chancellor of the Exchequer and First Lord of the Treasury, while his friend, Lord Townshend, once more became a Secretary of State. Although Walpole had never before been so powerful, he did not completely dominate the ministry nor was he generally recognized as Prime Minister. Sunderland and Carteret, who had been appointed as the other Secretary of State, still stood in his path.

Sunderland had been saved by Walpole in March 1721, but he was far from grateful. He resented the way he had been obliged to retreat from public office to the court appointment of Groom of the Stole, and he was jealous of Walpole's sudden climb up the political ladder. There was no way of challenging Walpole's authority at the Treasury or his influence in the Commons, but Sunderland made every effort to restrict Walpole's power elsewhere. At Court and in the conduct of diplomacy Sunderland and Carteret had greater influence than Walpole and Townshend. They also planned to use the King's patronage and the secret service funds to find more seats for their friends in the general election due in 1722. To this end, they used every form of flattery to win the support of the Duke of Newcastle, the greatest borough patron in the country. Many contemporaries believed Sunderland would get the better of his struggle with Walpole. Sunderland certainly laboured hard to outmanoeuvre Walpole in the general election of 1722, but the extent of his success was never put to the test. On 19 April 1722 he died, leaving Walpole in an even stronger position.

Walpole's ambitions had at last been crowned with success, and he remained in power for the next twenty years. During these years his ambition and his appetite for power never

I   Walpole with Speaker Onslow in the House of Commons
(c. 1730) – engraving by J. Fagg after Sir James Thornhill

III Thomas Pelham Holles, Duke of Newcastle – crayon drawing by William Hoare

II · Walpole in 1738 – bust by J. M. Rysbrack

waned. He was ruthless with those who challenged his authority, but it is not true that he disliked men of talent or wished to be surrounded by mere time-servers. Townshend could be rash and hot-headed, but he was an experienced diplomat with a mind of his own. The much-maligned Duke of Newcastle was not as foolish as he has often been portrayed. He had considerable knowledge of electoral, diplomatic, and administrative affairs. His brother, Henry Pelham, and his greatest friend, Philip Yorke, later Earl of Hardwicke, were men of undoubted talent and yet Walpole deliberately selected them for high office. He valued the services of these able men and only quarrelled with them when they desired to pursue policies which he regarded as mistaken or dangerous. Even then, he only forced Townshend out of office after considerable disagreements over the conduct of foreign policy and he made no effort to dismiss Newcastle and Hardwicke, though they caused him many headaches in the last years of his administration. With some determined and self-opinionated rivals, such as Carteret, Pulteney, and Bolingbroke, he took no chances, but with many others he preferred persuasion to wielding the big stick. Walpole was not so much jealous of talent as anxious to make the major political decisions himself. During the life of his administration he naturally faced many challenges and he suffered some reverses, but, before giving an account of his administration, it is important to examine how he maintained himself in power for so long and what methods his opponents used in their efforts to defeat him.

Walpole's domination of the political scene earned him the title of the 'Great Man' from both friends and enemies, and he was often described as the 'Prime Minister'. Though these were tributes to his power, they were also used by those jealous of his authority. While his position was certainly very strong, he did not have the power of a modern prime minister. He was in office primarily because the sovereign chose him, not because a party, a majority in Parliament, or a majority of the electorate wished the sovereign to ask him to form an administration. It did not mean, however, that because the sovereign asked him to serve at the head of the Treasury, he therefore had the constitutional privilege of choosing the other ministers to serve in the Government. All ministers were appointed by the Crown, and there was no guarantee that they would be loyal or subordinate to Walpole. His cabinets were collections of individuals. There was no cabinet solidarity. If a minister disagreed with Walpole yet retained the King's favour, then he was able to remain in the Government to continue his disputes with Walpole. When Walpole fell, the rest of his ministerial colleagues were free to continue in office. If he wished to dominate the ministry, therefore, Walpole had to persuade his colleagues to follow his lead or ask the King to remove them from office. Failing this, he had to struggle to get his policies accepted at Court, while other ministers campaigned to get their ideas across to the King.

In Parliament, particularly in the Commons, Walpole faced a similar situation. The votes of those who owed their seats or their offices to government patronage, namely the Court and Treasury party, and the general support of the Old Corps of the Whig party were not enough to give Walpole the kind of united, disciplined majority that a modern prime minister has in the House of Commons. Walpole had to concern himself much more with devising policies and arguments which would secure him the support of the independent backbenchers in Parliament. Only with their support could he be sure of a safe majority over his opponents, and so they needed to be carefully cultivated. Thus, Walpole's authority at Court, in the cabinet, and in Parliament rested far more on his personal ability to devise policies and persuade men to accept them, than on the kind of political power and patronage wielded by a modern prime minister.

Only Walpole's bitterest enemies were blind to the fact that he possessed these personal qualities to a greater degree than any of his contemporaries. His most prejudiced opponents claimed that he survived in office only because of the arbitrary and ill-judged decision of the King and because of the corrupt methods he himself used to buy support in Parliament. These accusations, while not without a grain of truth in them, failed to recognize Walpole's political talents and so made the task of defeating him more difficult. Many contemporaries, however, and almost all historians have acknowledged Walpole's capabilities. Lord Hervey, a colleague who did not always flatter Walpole in his *Memoirs*, praised his coolness, his judgement, and his insight into the nature of mankind. Walpole, he maintained, learned the strength and weaknesses of most men so that he knew how best to persuade them or to resist them without driving them into opposition. His years of power and the heavy responsibilities of his high office did not prevent him being cheerful, friendly, and approachable. His realism and his pragmatism made him avoid all policies which were grandiose in theory but impossible to implement. These qualities also made him retreat when he met overwhelming opposition to his plans. His indefatigable energy and his methodical application to business made him formidable, particularly in financial matters, though, later, he also became very knowledgeable about foreign affairs. Lord Chesterfield, who spent most of his political career in opposition

to Walpole, could still praise some of Walpole's personal qualities when he came to write his *Characters of Eminent Personages of His Own Time*. He criticized Walpole for his immorality,
his corrupt practices, his excessive love of flattery, and his
limited political vision, but he confessed that Walpole was good-
natured, frank, and affable, that he had the extraordinary ability
of explaining the most intricate matters to the satisfaction of
the most ignorant backbenchers, and that he was the ablest
manager of Parliament who had ever lived.

The assessments of Hervey and Chesterfield were very near
the mark. Walpole remained in power for more than twenty
years because he had an unrivalled ability to manage men and
a profound understanding of how the political system which
developed after 1714 actually worked. Whether he was discussing politics with his sovereign or with his cabinet colleagues,
whether he was addressing a small group of M.P.s or the whole
House of Commons, he had an unerring instinct for the mood
of his audience, for the tone he should adopt, and for the arguments which would prove most persuasive. None of his contemporaries could match his skill in carrying others with him
or his cool assessment of when to give ground without being
routed. Nor could anyone rival his ability at rewarding one
political or economic interest without alienating a more powerful group. During his years in power he won the support of
the Dissenting and financial interests without driving the Church
and landed interests into opposition. Furthermore, in his appreciation of the real sources of power he had no equal. He accepted
the fact that it was his sovereign who put him into office, but
he knew that without the support of the Commons he could
not remain in power very long.

It was his clear realization that he must push the Court's
policies through the Commons while also representing the
views of the majority of the House at Court that made him such
an effective link between Crown and Parliament. While he
knew that he depended upon the confidence of both King and
Commons, he also learned how to use his influence on both of
them in turn in order to increase his power over the other.

Thus, his hold over the King enabled him to exploit the Crown's patronage as a means of building up a body of loyal supporters in Parliament and to decide what policies had the best chance of securing the support of a majority in the Commons. Conversely, his ability to persuade a majority in the Commons to meet the financial needs of the Government enabled him to ingratiate himself with his royal master. In 1727, for example, he strongly recommended himself to George II because of his success in persuading the Commons to vote the new King an increased civil list and to grant Queen Caroline a separate income of £100,000 *per annum*. Walpole therefore clearly understood the delicate and complicated interaction between one element of the political structure and another. He appreciated that, in order to stay in power, he had to manage all the elements in the system at the same time. For the sake of clarity, however, we need to examine separately his skill in handling the five main components of the political system: the Court, the cabinet, the parliamentary constituencies, the Court and Treasury party, and the independent backbenchers.

In order to gain, let alone stay in, power the first requirement was influence at Court. Walpole needed to persuade the King to reward the candidates for office whom he recommended and to accept the policies which he proposed. This meant that Walpole had to learn the arts of court intrigue and make sure that his arguments carried most weight with the King. One means to this end was simply to exploit his direct access to the King as head of the Treasury. Since Walpole was renowned for his persuasive tongue and the force and clarity of his opinions, this was sometimes enough to carry the day. He could not always rely on the King being in a receptive mood, however, and so he was forced to employ other methods. One approach was to have his ideas repeated to the King by other people with influence at Court. In George I's reign Walpole bribed the King's German mistresses, particularly the Duchess of Kendal, to support his case. When George II came to the throne, Walpole wisely realized that Queen Caroline had more influence on the King in political matters than any of his mistresses. As he crudely put it, he seized 'the right sow by the ear'. Walpole would discuss political matters quite frankly with the Queen and often she was able to cajole her husband into following his advice, even though the King was not prepared to listen directly or personally to his minister's arguments. After Queen Caroline's death in 1737 Walpole had to rely on the assistance of the King's daughters and his favourite mistress, Madame Walmoden, who was brought over from Hanover. Unfortunately for him, they could not match the late Queen's political influence on George II.

Throughout his years in power Walpole also tried to safeguard his influence at Court by restricting the number of those who had direct access to the sovereign. Of course he could not stop mistresses, royal favourites, and courtiers discussing politics with the King, and sometimes their activities created political problems for him. Walpole therefore was not always able to prevail against the advice of others at Court, and he certainly could not dictate to his sovereign. Both the first two Hanoverian monarchs were stubborn, had autocratic temperaments, and were devoted to the interests of their native electorate. They were particularly sensitive about their prerogative to appoint men to high office, to control the army, and to conduct foreign policy. When he discussed these topics at Court Walpole always had to tread warily. He could never be certain that his friends would be appointed to important offices or that his dangerous rivals would be dismissed, though in most instances, after wearisome discussions with the King, he succeeded. At no time, however, did he control military matters. George I preferred the advice of General Cadogan, whereas George II believed that no one knew as much about military affairs as himself, and so he would accept advice from no one. In discussions on the conduct of foreign policy Walpole had to combat not only the advice of some of his ministerial colleagues, but the opinions of his sovereign. He could never afford to let the King believe that he was prepared to sacrifice the interests or the honour of Hanover. Carteret almost replaced Walpole in the confidence of George

I in 1723 by appearing more concerned about Hanoverian affairs than his rival. In 1734 Walpole had to exert all his influence to prevent George II and Queen Caroline from following their inclination to enter the War of the Polish Succession to protect the honour of Hanover and safeguard the interests of the Emperor. In the event his advice was grudgingly accepted, but he suffered so much anxiety that he must often have smiled ruefully at the charge that his word was law at Court. In fact, in this instance, he only kept the country out of the war by agreeing to increase the size of the army. He would willingly have spared himself both the unpopularity of voting for such a large force and the trouble of finding the necessary revenue to maintain it, but he decided it was better to flatter the King in this way than embark on a major war in Europe.

The Court was only one source of political power. In order to stay in power Walpole had to translate royal favour into control over the ministry and, consequently, over the policies brought before Parliament. In particular, he had to prevent his ministerial colleagues having too many opportunities to suggest to the King policies that he himself opposed. To this end he deliberately dispensed with large, rather formal, cabinet meetings where the King might receive conflicting advice or be able to choose between the different policies advocated by his ministers. Instead, real power was concentrated in the hands of a small group of ministers who were trusted by Walpole. This inner cabinet, which usually consisted of Walpole, the two Secretaries of State, the Lord Chancellor, and the Lord President of the Council, met frequently but informally to decide the broad outlines of policy. Other ministers and experts in particular fields might be called in to give advice, but they did not make decisions. In some of these discussions, particularly on foreign affairs, Walpole found himself in a minority, but, because he was the only commoner and the only finance minister in the cabinet and therefore had the sole responsibility for pushing the Government's policies through the Commons, these defeats were few in number. Once this inner cabinet came to a decision the King was approached, usually by Walpole him-

self, and was offered the cabinet's advice. Only when this advice
had been accepted, did the larger, formal cabinet council meet
to ratify the policy that had already been decided.

Even during the King's annual visits to Hanover, Walpole
was able to restrict the number of those offering advice. The
King was always accompanied by one of the Secretaries of State,
and Walpole could generally, though not always, trust
Townshend and Harrington, who made most of these trips to
Hanover. In the King's absence, authority was officially invested
in the Lords Justices, who were simply the formal cabinet council under another name. Nevertheless, it was still the inner
cabinet which made all the important decisions. When George
II was in Hanover, he usually left Queen Caroline with almost
full regal authority and so made Walpole's task even easier.
Despite all his precautions, however, Walpole could not prevent
his ministerial colleagues approaching the King with advice
which he disliked. He broke with Carteret and Townshend, and
had many quarrels with Newcastle, because these ministers, as
Secretaries of State, disagreed with his ideas on the conduct of
foreign policy.

In order to assert his personal authority over the ministry,
Walpole forced dangerous rivals, such as Carteret and
Townshend, out of office, kept potential rivals, such as Pulteney
and Bolingbroke out of office altogether, and made sure that his
most loyal supporters, such as Henry Pelham, Philip Yorke, and
Dudley Ryder, were conspicuously rewarded. This practice was
observed not only with regard to the ministry in London, but
also in the administration of Scotland and Ireland. In 1725 the
Duke of Roxburgh, the Secretary of State for Scotland, who was
one of Carteret's political allies, made little effort to prevent,
and may even have incited, the Shawfield rioters in Glasgow,
who protested at Walpole's attempt to impose a duty on malt
in Scotland. Walpole struck back ruthlessly. He persuaded the
King to dismiss Roxburgh, to abolish his office, and to break his
power in Scotland. Henceforth he relied on the Argyll interest
to manage Scottish affairs. The Duke of Argyll, the most influential peer in Scotland, was too proud and irascible to take orders

from Walpole, and in 1737 he went into opposition. Fortunately his interest and the Government's patronage in Scotland was controlled by his brother, the Earl of Islay, who proved himself a better manager and a more pliable courtier. Walpole did not directly control Scotland, but, in conjunction with Islay, he became the most powerful influence in Scottish politics. In Ireland the opposition to William Wood's royal patent to mint small copper coins became so great that between 1722 and 1725 the Irish Privy Council and the Irish Parliament rebelled against the dictates of the Government in London. Walpole had to give way to Irish pressure in this instance, but his defeat only made him redouble his efforts to bring the Irish administration under his control. He persuaded the King to appoint loyal English peers to the chief legal posts in Ireland and to translate Hugh Boulter from the see of Bristol to the primacy of all Ireland as Archbishop of Armagh. Boulter then laboured to build up an interest in Ireland that was subservient to Walpole. All patronage was dispensed in return for political loyalty. 'Undertakers' or borough-mongers, who secured a complaisant Irish Parliament for the Government, were rewarded with suitable pensions and lucrative offices.

It was by such means that Walpole demonstrated to the world the considerable credit he had at Court. Those who supported him could expect to reap material rewards. He himself openly displayed the vast wealth which he had acquired in office. Some of it almost certainly came by illicit means, though this could never be proved because his King and his colleagues protected him. The legitimate proceeds of his public offices could not have provided Walpole with the huge sums needed to build his magnificent new palace at Houghton in Norfolk. This was decorated by the greatest craftsmen of the day and filled with beautiful furniture and paintings. Walpole regularly lavished expensive hospitality on his friends, both at Houghton and at his other homes in London. In addition to his own vast rewards, Walpole made sure that his family and friends reaped some of the fruits of his power. His brothers, his sons, and even his mistress, Maria Skerrett, were given offices, sinecures, or pensions. He also found posts in the Treasury for old friends and clients, such as Robert Mann and Thomas Cremer. As they learned to recognize Walpole as the real source of patronage, or at least as the channel through which most of it flowed, ambitious politicians such as Thomas Winnington and Henry Fox, though they came of Tory stock, offered to serve him.

Because he was the dominant influence at Court and in the cabinet and because he was the head of the Treasury and the unofficial leader of the House of Commons, Walpole was able to control a great deal of crown patronage. He deliberately exploited this in order to build up a dependable body of supporters in the constituencies and in Parliament. Since it was possible to translate crown patronage into political power, Walpole naturally sought to increase and engross the various means of rewarding those who would support him. The demand for government favours always exceeded the supply. Walpole was often heard to complain that there was not enough grass for the beasts to feed on. Nevertheless, by judicious management Walpole eventually controlled a wider field of patronage than any previous royal minister had ever thought was possible. By dispensing this, with the King's approval, he was able to build up a powerful Court and Treasury party which helped him to win elections and assisted him in managing Parliament.

The sovereign had at his disposal the highest positions and honours in the land. He awarded peerages and other marks of social distinction and he appointed all the major officials at Court and in the Government. These rewards were limited in number, though Walpole deliberately widened the scope by reviving the Order of the Bath. Most of the rewards of this type went to the most loyal and influential politicians, but there was a vast range of lesser patronage in the administration and in the professions that could be used to influence voters or Members of Parliament. All government departments, but particularly those responsible to the Treasury, employed large numbers of officials and also awarded many profitable contracts to supply the armed forces with food and equipment. Walpole deliberately set out to bring all this patronage under his personal control. John Scrope, the highly efficient Secretary to the Treasury from 1724 to 1752, helped Walpole to gain control over all the officials in the Scottish revenue service after the suppression of the office of Secretary of State for Scotland in 1725. Scrope also engineered and carried through Walpole's policy of appointing even minor local officials in the revenue service. The Treasury gradually spread its influence to every area where the revenue departments were active. Since the revenue officers in the customs and excise service needed to be efficient and experienced, they were not appointed or promoted solely on political grounds, but they were expected to be loyal to the Government once in office. Walpole concerned himself with even minor appointments because there were plenty of men with political influence seeking some kind of reward for their relatives and clients. In 1730 Walpole decided to please the Commons by abolishing the salt duty, but he then discovered that he had put nearly three hundred and fifty salt-duty commissioners out of a job and had thereby inadvertently reduced the amount of patronage at his disposal. Two years later he decided to revive the salt duty, partly in order to restore the number of appointments under his control. Whenever the Opposition sought to reduce the number of placemen and pensioners at his disposal, Walpole recognized this as a threat to his political influence and always engineered the defeat of these measures.

Apart from the numerous appointments and contracts made by the administrative departments, there was a vast range of crown patronage in the major professions, the law, the armed forces, and the Church. The most important legal officers in England, Scotland and Ireland, including the Lord Chancellor, the Lord Chief Justice, the Solicitor-General and the Attorney-General, the Lord Advocate, and the Lord Justice Clerk, were all political appointments, and they all eventually came under Walpole's influence. Even Lords-Lieutenant and Justices of the Peace were expected to prove their political reliability; or at least, they risked losing their positions if they opposed the Government. Walpole never gained such personal influence over the commissioning and promotion of officers in the army and navy, because both George I and George II were reluctant to delegate this power. Nevertheless, he tried to ensure that those who offered advice to the King on such matters were his political friends. He persuaded George I to appoint Henry Pelham as Secretary at War and the Duke of Argyll as Commander-in-Chief in place of one of his opponents, General Cadogan. When George II came to the throne he was able to secure the dismissal of Lord Berkeley, one of his critics, as head of the Admiralty and to pack the admiralty board with his own creatures.

One of Walpole's most important successes was the achievement of a greater measure of control over promotions within the Church of England. The Church had a greater share in shaping men's opinions than any other institution, but too often in the past it had used its influence on behalf of the Tory party. Although Walpole could not prevent most of the ordinary parish clergy opposing or criticizing his administration, he did have considerable influence over those who looked to the Crown for advancement. Many hundreds of livings were in the gift of the Crown. These were dispensed by the Lord Chancellor, who, though always a Whig, was not always entirely subservient to Walpole. Nevertheless, these appointments never went to outspoken critics of Walpole's administration. Walpole had more influence over those clerics who desired to become Royal Chaplains, or to hold the new Regius Professorships in history and languages that were established at Oxford and Cambridge, or to climb the church hierarchy. It certainly became clear that elevation to the episcopacy depended upon political influence, and no one carried more weight than Walpole when these decisions were taken. Walpole had no wish to antagonize the Church and so he was ready to promote sound, even excellent, churchmen, but only if they were politically reliable. Since he could not rely upon the support of the two archbishops, who were in office before he came to power, he turned for advice about clerical preferments to Edmund Gibson, Bishop of London. He soon became known as 'Walpole's Pope'. From 1723, when he first offered his services, until his breach with Walpole in 1736, when he tried to take an independent line on church affairs, Gibson helped the Government to secure a bench of bishops that was politically loyal. Gibson and Walpole were not always successful in their recommendations because there was considerable political manoeuvring over such important positions and many people took an interest in their bestowal. Queen Caroline, for example, secured the promotion of Thomas Sherlock to successive bishoprics in 1728 and 1734, while Lord Hervey helped Dr Butts become Bishop of Norwich in 1733. Unlike Sherlock, Butts was at least a reliable Walpolean Whig. In most instances, however, the men recommended by Gibson and backed by Walpole were promoted. In 1723 alone, six bishoprics fell vacant and, by translating some men from poorer to richer sees, Walpole was able to reward nine Whig churchmen put forward by Gibson. Within a few years the bench of bishops was dominated by the clerical supporters of Walpole.

Walpole devoted so much time and energy to extending and dispensing crown patronage because of the political support it undoubtedly brought him. The political influence of the Treasury and Admiralty helped to elect perhaps as many as thirty or forty Government supporters to the House of Commons. In very few constituencies was the government interest so strong that it could control both seats, but in a number of boroughs it was the stronger interest and in others it was the deciding factor. It was most powerful in treasury boroughs such as Harwich and Orford, in admiralty boroughs such as Plymouth, Portsmouth, and Rochester, and in those constituencies where royal officials had considerable influence, such as the Cinque Ports and the boroughs of the Isle of Wight. In addition, Walpole could count upon the support of borough patrons who were attached to the government interest by other forms of patronage. He and Townshend had built up a considerable interest in Norfolk, the Duke of Newcastle owned a couple of pocket-boroughs and was powerful throughout Sussex, the Duke of Devonshire was influential in Derbyshire and the Duke of Rutland in Leicestershire, Richard Edgcumbe had a secure interest in several Cornish boroughs, while the Argyll faction was the strongest electoral interest in Scotland. Walpole appreciated the value of such men and so he shrewdly established a network of patrons and election-managers to exert influence in every area of the country. These men carefully nursed their constituencies: the voters were flattered, entertained, and constantly reminded of the powerful personal and government interest which could be either used for their benefit or withheld from them.

These were the recognized methods of building up an electoral interest, but Walpole and his friends were not beyond using more corrupt means to influence election results. Large sums of money from the secret service fund, for example, were dispensed during general election campaigns. There is clear evidence that in 1727 considerable cash inducements were offered to the small electorates in a number of Cornish boroughs. In 1734, when the ministry faced a crucial general election campaign, Walpole's disbursement of secret service money reached its peak. When the Opposition in the Commons protested against such corrupt practices, Walpole strenuously defended his agents from these attacks. In February 1722 he successfully protected Sir Francis Page, an exchequer official, against a charge that he had attempted the wholesale bribery of the electors of Banbury. Walpole was evidently more concerned about the size of his majority than the morality of his methods.

After every general election he was able to increase his majority by ensuring that most disputed elections were decided in favour of the candidate supported by the ministry. In December 1741 his imminent fall was heralded by his narrow failure to have his candidate elected as chairman of the Committee of Privileges and Elections which considered such disputed election results. Two months later he resigned, after more than twenty years in power, when the Commons decided that the candidates he thought the House should accept as the Members for Chippenham should be turned out in favour of two of his opponents. It seemed a small issue to end a great career, but the decision clearly showed that he had lost the confidence of the Commons. While he remained in power, Walpole took full advantage of the system of infrequent and costly elections and rarely-contested seats that favoured the strong government interest. Every attempt by his opponents to return to triennial general elections, to pass Acts designed to end bribery and corruption in elections, or to ensure that all candidates possessed the right property qualifications, was opposed by Walpole. When one Act to prevent bribery and corruption in elections was passed by Parliament in May 1736, Walpole made sure that its terms were never put into effect.

The election of government candidates was the first, but by no means the only means of building up the Court and Treasury party in Parliament. The vast range of crown patronage was used to reward those who voluntarily supported the administration or to persuade other Members of Parliament to follow the Government's lead. It was not only dispensed to make men dependent on the ministry, but also to create goodwill among those whose support might be needed in a crucial division. Patronage was particularly effective in the Lords, where Walpole was able to secure a permanent majority. The nobility believed that they ought to play a major role in governing the country and they were less willing than many Members of the Commons to resign themselves to long years in opposition. Most of them were therefore ready to serve the Crown and Walpole, in return for important positions at Court and leading posts in the administration. Walpole, in fact, was the only commoner with real influence at Court and genuine power in the ministry. Should the Lords show themselves reluctant to support the policies of Walpole, the Crown's favourite minister, then the King could alter the composition of the Upper House. He had the power to create new peers. In 1734, for example, when Walpole's hold on the Lords seemed to be slipping, George II elevated four of Walpole's supporters to the peerage as Lords Hinton, Talbot, Hervey, and Hardwicke. The Government could also influence the election of the sixteen Scottish peers. In 1734, by a system of rewards and promises, the ministry's entire list of sixteen representatives for Scotland was chosen by the Scottish peerage. Finally, Walpole could increasingly rely on the support of the twenty-six bishops in the Lords because he and Gibson recommended none but loyal Government Whigs for these high clerical honours. In 1733, when Walpole was fighting for his political life and when, for the first time during his administration, his control of the Lords was threatened, he was saved by the loyalty of the bishops. The Opposition sought to embarrass the Government by pressing for an inquiry into the disposal of the confiscated estates of the former directors of the South Sea Company. In the most crucial division the Lords were equally divided with seventy-five votes cast on either side, and the Opposition's motion was eventually lost. No less than twenty-four bishops voted for the ministerial side. Archbishop Wake was absent because of illness and failed to leave a proxy vote, while only one bishop supported the Opposition. Since the House of Lords was rarely so well attended, the Government could count upon its friends to defeat such popular, but politically embarrassing, measures as the Place and Pension Bills which it sometimes feared to oppose in the Commons. When a number of court peers voiced their objections to Walpole's excise scheme in 1733, he made sure that many of them were taught a lesson. Although the Excise Bill never reached the Lords, Walpole persuaded George II to dismiss from their offices and places those peers who had threatened to defect, '*pour encourager les autres*'.

In the Commons the government interest was not so dominant as in the Lords. The greatest rewards largely went to the peers, while much of the minor forms of crown patronage, such as posts in the revenue service, went to oblige the clients or distant relatives of the aristocracy or to influence the electorate in some constituencies. Even when these small favours were given to Members of the Commons, or to their relatives, clients, or constituents, they were not sufficient reward to make these Members give up their cherished political independence and become servile creatures of the ministry. The Government could only ensure that these Members did not go into permanent opposition along with those determined Country backbenchers who refused any favour from the Government lest it should appear that they had abandoned their principles. The Court and Treasury party, which was expected to vote for the Govern-

IV   George II in middle life –
painting by
John Shackleton

V   Queen Caroline – painting
by Enoch Seeman

VI   'Ready Mony the prevailing Candidate, or the Humours of an Election' (1727) – an attack on the corrupt practices used during the general election of 1727

ment's measures, was therefore restricted to those Members who were returned by the Government's electoral interest or who signalled their dependence on the Crown by accepting a regular income from office, place, or pension. The size and discipline of this Court and Treasury party has often been exaggerated. It probably did not number much above 120 members in the Commons. The number of placemen had not increased very much since Anne's reign, but the marked decline in the pull of party loyalty, and Walpole's determination to enforce discipline, forced a higher percentage of these men into the Government's lobby. Walpole could not afford to enforce rigid discipline when these Members were not totally dependent on crown patronage for their livelihood, but he expected them to toe the line on crucial divisions. In 1737 Sir George Oxenden, a member of the Court and Treasury party for more than ten years, was turned out of his place on the treasury board because he supported the Opposition's demand for an increased personal allowance for Prince Frederick when it was clear that George II resented this claim being made.

Even if the professional, front-bench politicians holding government office are added to the numbers of the Court and Treasury party, the administration could not control more than about 150 votes in the Commons. Only in very badly attended debates, therefore, could Walpole be confident of a majority. For much of the time, and on all important measures, Walpole required the support of many of the independent backbenchers. For more than twenty years, except for a few notable instances, Walpole persuaded enough independent backbenchers to support his policies. He won the confidence of the Commons partly by his expert management of its Members and partly by a shrewd assessment of what measures the majority would be prepared to tolerate. It was this achievement which made him the greatest minister of the Crown in the first half of the eighteenth century.

Walpole's opponents were always ready to complain about his extensive use of crown patronage. They tended to exaggerate the size of the Court and Treasury party and to underestimate

Walpole's success in winning the confidence of the independent backbenchers. Later historians have been more generous in their recognition of Walpole's ability to manage the Commons, but they have rarely explained the methods he used. His success in fact depended primarily on four means of satisfying the independent backbenchers: his care in presenting the ministry's case; his expert knowledge and skilful use of parliamentary procedure; his readiness to respect the opinions of the average backbencher; and, finally, his willingness to retreat when he could not carry the majority of the Commons with him.

When he had agreed upon the Government's policies with the King and his ministerial colleagues, Walpole made certain that these decisions were explained in detail to as many Members as possible. Before the beginning of each session and prior to every important debate, Walpole entertained to dinner between twenty and thirty of his chief supporters and influential backbenchers in the Commons. At these gatherings he refrained from laying down the law, but sought to give the impression that he was willing to listen to advice and to amend the policies under discussion. His lieutenants, and sometimes a few independent backbenchers, would then sound out a wider cross-section of Members. Finally, Walpole would call a mass meeting of his potential supporters at the Cockpit, a government building in Whitehall. Sometimes more than two hundred Members gathered to hear him. Once more he would explain his policies and defend or amend them as seemed necessary. This approach invariably worked, and it was triumphantly vindicated in April 1733. Then, the Opposition, having forced Walpole to abandon his Excise Bill, decided to press for the election of a committee of twenty-one Members to inquire into the alleged abuses in the customs service. If his opponents had been able to elect their list of candidates for this committee, they would have made strenuous efforts to convict Walpole of corrupt practices. Walpole, however, even with his back to the wall, proved a far better political manager than his opponents. He summoned a meeting of his potential supporters at the Cockpit, and no fewer than 263 Members turned up to hear him. The Opposition, he claimed, was not really interested in discovering any failings in the operation of the customs service, but aimed to overthrow the administration. Could they afford to trust a group which was supported by so many Tory backbenchers and was incited by Bolingbroke, who had served the Pretender during the 1715 rebellion? Could they risk the defeat of a ministry dedicated to the Revolution Settlement and the Hanoverian succession? The answer was given next day. The huge number of 503 Members attended the election of the committee of inquiry, and the majority supported Walpole's list of twenty-one placemen. Not surprisingly, a committee composed of such men failed to discover any evidence of malpractices in the customs service.

Walpole did not take such precautions only before each session opened or in political emergencies. Throughout his career he employed Members such as Henry Pelham, Thomas Winnington, Thomas Brereton, and his own brother, Horatio, to inform, consult, and cajole individual backbenchers. He himself was often observed in the chamber holding conversations with backbenchers in a last minute attempt to get them to support the ministry on the issue actually being debated on the floor of the Commons. Walpole made these efforts because he knew that a great many backbenchers genuinely prided themselves on their political independence. They were not committed to either side beforehand, but were ready to be swayed by what they heard. This meant that the actual debates in the Commons had a greater influence on the final voting than in more recent times, when Members are usually committed to a particular line by their party allegiance. Walpole therefore took immense trouble in marshalling the ministry's case for the debates in the Commons. He himself spoke in nearly every important debate throughout his whole period in power. Sometimes he introduced measures or motions personally, though he more often allowed his lieutenants to open the debate while he waited to sum up for the Government after he had gauged the mood and weighed the opinions of the backbenchers. Less eloquent than William Pulteney, one of his leading critics, Walpole was nevertheless a lucid and forceful speaker. He took great pains to make sure that the Commons was never in any doubt as to why he was advocating a particular policy. The same could be said of his principal lieutenants in the Commons. The ministry's front-bench speakers made a formidable debating team. Walpole has often been accused of employing the subservient and the second-rate. This is a poor description of his lieutenants in the Commons when he was able to call on the services of Henry Pelham, Horatio Walpole, John Scrope, Thomas Winnington, Sir William Strickland, Sir Charles Wager, and Sir William Yonge. The Opposition might sneer at the ability of these men, who were not, it must be admitted, dazzling performers; but they were indefatigable in their attendance, well-briefed in their particular fields of knowledge, and clear in their exposition of the Government's case. They were more than a match for some of the eloquent speakers for the Opposition.

Since he could not be certain that the force of the ministry's arguments would always provide him with a majority, Walpole was ready to manipulate the procedure of the House of Commons to his advantage. He could do this partly because none of his contemporaries was able to match his knowledge of parliamentary procedure and partly because the ministry had considerable advantages in the conduct of business in the Commons. The Government's normal majority generally allowed it to elect as Speaker and chairman of the committees of the House men who could be relied upon to favour the ministry should this prove necessary. Spencer Compton, the Speaker from 1715 to 1727, was not a great supporter of Walpole, but, since he was also Paymaster of the Forces after 1722, he was not in a position to use his influence to obstruct the ministry's business in the Commons. He concentrated instead on winning the friendship of the Prince of Wales in the hope that he might replace Walpole at the head of the ministry when George I died. Arthur Onslow, who was chosen as the Speaker in 1728 and who held the post until 1761, boasted of his political independence and was generally respected by the Opposition. Nevertheless, he was clearly the Court's candidate for the post and he was quite prepared to combine the Speakership with an office under the Crown, for he was Treasurer of the Navy from 1734 to 1742. He did have an occasional dispute with Walpole, but, by asserting his independence in these instances, he proved all the more valuable when he did side with the administration. Thus, Onslow sympathized with the Opposition in their attacks on bribery and the size of the standing army, but this did not prevent him assisting the ministry in a whole variety of ways.

This could often be done unobtrusively by enforcing the dignity of the House, keeping order during debates, preventing any unnecessary obstruction or delay of public business, and advising the ministers on matters of procedure. Onslow usually attended the meetings Walpole held before each session and prior to every major debate. On these occasions he offered his advice on what he believed would be acceptable to the Commons. In one meeting in December 1732 he spoke out strongly against any plea to bring in a bill to repeal the Test and Corporation Acts because he was certain that this would inflame the whole House. When called upon, however, the Speaker's sympathy with the administration was made more apparent. He knew which Government spokesmen to call upon in any debate and at the end of most discussions in the Commons he would decide the question in favour of the ministry, thus throwing the responsibility for forcing any division on the Opposition. When the House was in committee the Speaker was out of the chair and allowed to vote. In March 1733 Onslow voted in favour of Walpole's Excise Bill even though it was running into heavy opposition at the time and later had to be abandoned. The Speaker could vote from the chair when his casting vote was needed to break a deadlock, and on one celebrated occasion Onslow used this privilege to protect Walpole. In March 1742, shortly after Walpole's fall, the Commons elected a committee to investigate the minister's conduct during his last ten years in office. Four Members tied for the last two places on this committee and Onslow was able to choose the two who were well-disposed towards Walpole instead of two outspoken critics. In this case he was compelled to make a decision. On another occasion he went out of his way to assist Walpole against his opponents. When Walpole called the famous meeting at the Cockpit, in April 1733, to advise his supporters against letting the Opposition elect their candidates to the committee of inquiry into the abuses in the customs service, Onslow not only attended, but spoke in favour of the ministry's list of candidates and supported Walpole's argument that it would be dangerous to let the Opposition overthrow the administration.

The Speaker would not have been so valuable to Walpole in these emergencies if he had not been allowed to demonstrate his relative independence at other times. From the chairman of the committees of the Commons, however, Walpole demanded a more subservient attitude towards the ministry. To ensure this he strove to have members of the Court and Treasury party elected to chair the most important committees, particularly the vital Committee of Privileges and Elections. When Walpole failed to elect his candidate to the chairmanship of this committee in December 1741, he knew that he was losing control of the Commons. Other committees of the House were usually chaired by the Member who introduced the relevant bill or motion, though Walpole had no scruples about overruling this convention when necessary. In 1729 he opposed Sir John Barnard's claim to be chosen as the chairman of a committee to examine complaints about Spanish attacks on British merchant ships in West Indian waters, even though Barnard had initiated the inquiry. Walpole knew that Barnard, the Opposition's leading spokesman on financial and commercial matters, would seek to bring forward resolutions critical of the ministry's handling of this issue. Since he was anxious that the Commons should not take decisions which would strain Britain's relations with Spain, he secured the election of Thomas Winnington, a dependable placeman. With Winnington in the chair the inquiry was hamstrung. At one meeting of the committee Winnington deliberately ignored Barnard's attempts to speak and turned instead to a supporter of the ministry. His partial behaviour prevented Barnard proposing any motions critical of the administration and the Opposition Members walked out of the committee in disgust.

The Opposition had to endure this kind of partiality by the chairman of committees on several occasions. In January 1723 Phillips Gybbon, the chairman of the Committee of Privileges and Elections, gave his opinion that the ayes had it when the ministry moved to adjourn a debate which was proving embarrassing. When the Opposition demanded that votes should actually be counted, Gybbon leaped out of the chair, claiming that this could not be done as the doors of the chamber were not locked as required before a division. By this ignoble pretext Walpole's administration avoided the risk of defeat. It cheated the Opposition of another chance of success in February 1730 when a committee was debating the evidence on the rebuilding of the fortifications of Dunkirk, contrary to the terms of the Treaty of Utrecht. The Opposition planned to introduce a motion condemning the Government for allowing these fortifications to be restored by the French. Walpole preferred a milder motion, which would respectfully ask the King to secure a promise from the French Government that any unauthorized fortifications at Dunkirk would be destroyed. Even though Sir William Wyndham introduced the Opposition's motion first, the chairman of the committee, Richard Edgcumbe, a placeman and a close friend of Walpole, deliberately ignored Wyndham's seconder, who was on his feet, and allowed the ministry to propose and second its counter-proposal. When this motion was carried, the Opposition could not proceed with its alternative proposal.

During his years in power Walpole also learned to exploit other forms of parliamentary procedure to his advantage. When the Opposition proposed resolutions, bills, or inquiries that were likely to prove popular with the independent backbenchers, Walpole hesitated to demand the outright rejection of these proposals. He resorted instead to other means of avoiding a direct confrontation, which could result in a humiliating defeat or at least might risk offending the sensibilities of the backbenchers. He sometimes allowed such popular measures as Place and Pension Bills to pass the Commons, knowing that they could be rejected more easily in the Lords. On other occasions he

amended bills to make them less popular or voted for an adjourn-
ment of a debate. If he was uncertain of the strength of feeling
in the chamber, he tested opinion by dividing the Commons on
whether the question should now be put to the House, instead of
dividing on the actual question itself. When he feared that his
own measures might run into heavy opposition, Walpole used
a variety of techniques to avoid losing the confidence of the
Commons. With some bills, such as his famous excise scheme
of 1733, that were proving immensely unpopular, he prevented
the Opposition having the satisfaction of rejecting them by
moving that the next reading should be put off for so long that
the session would be over before there was any chance of pro-
ceeding with these measures. Some unpopular measures, such
as the bill introduced in April 1723 to impose a special tax on
Roman Catholics, were delayed until near the end of the session
in the hope that many backbenchers would not be able to vote
because they had left London for their estates. In other instances,
Walpole tried to wear down the opposition by letting debates
drag on long into the night or even very late into the session
in the hope that the backbench squires would tire of the issue
and give up attending the House.

The most important example of this tactic occurred over
the Dunkirk inquiry of 1730. When the Opposition revealed that
the French had broken their treaty obligations by rebuilding
the defences of this port, Walpole knew he would have to play
for time to allow the passions of the independent backbenchers
to cool. He shrewdly avoided a division by asking the Members
to wait until Colonel Armstrong had returned from an inspec-
tion of Dunkirk and until all the relevant diplomatic papers had
been laid before the House. This gave him a breathing-space of
two weeks. He used this time to deluge the Commons with
copies of the Government's letters to France on the subject,
though not of course with the evasive replies, and to lobby the
backbenchers against taking the word of Bolingbroke in this
dispute. When the debate was resumed, many waverers renewed
their support of the ministry. Nevertheless, as has already been
shown, Walpole took care to ensure that the Commons voted

on the ministry's proposal that the King should continue his efforts to get any unauthorized fortifications demolished rather than on the Opposition's motion to censure the Government.

Walpole therefore had no scruples about manipulating the procedures of the Commons if this could extricate him from the risk of defeat, but on many occasions he carried the independent backbenchers with him because he respected their opinions and acknowledged their power. Bubb Dodington ridiculed Walpole for taking as much care in dressing for the Commons as he would if he were going to visit his mistress, but this merely illustrated that Walpole was the first royal minister fully to appreciate the importance of the Commons and the wisdom of flattering its Members. On two occasions in 1739, when he was fighting for his political life, he frankly told the Commons that he survived in office only so long as he enjoyed the confidence of the majority of the Members. He would therefore always seek to make his policies acceptable to them. On 1 February 1739 he declared:

A seat in this House is equal to any dignity derived from posts or titles, and the approbation of this House is preferable to all that power, or even Majesty itself, can bestow: therefore when I speak here as a minister, I speak as possessing my powers from His Majesty, but as being answerable to this House for the exercise of those powers.

Later that year, on 21 November, he confessed:

I have lived long enough in the world, Sir, to know that the safety of a minister lies in his having the approbation of this House. Former ministers, Sir, neglected this, and therefore they fell; I have always made it my first study to obtain it, and therefore I hope to stand.

Walpole did not attempt this flattery merely because he was running into heavy opposition in 1739. Throughout his career he concentrated much of his energies on his performance in the Commons. Although he was a busy minister, the frequency of his attendance in the chamber and the number of times he addressed the House could match that of any of his contemporaries, none of whom had as many other heavy responsibilities. Moreover, he never stood aloof from the ordinary Member. He was approachable and he always carefully explained himself, even to the most dim-witted squire. He deliberately projected himself as the bluff, honest country gentleman, who was in tune with the feelings and opinions of the average backbencher. Even when under heavy pressure, he was invariably tolerant and good-humoured. When William Shippen, the Jacobite, criticized Walpole in a debate in January 1730 and observed that 'it was for the benefit of the Ministers [for Members] to find fault, for the more they were rubbed, the brighter they would be', Walpole replied smartly, 'If so, I must be the brightest minister that ever was.'

Walpole's successful management of the Commons ultimately rested on his willingness to abandon unpopular measures and on his readiness to pursue policies which a majority of Members would be prepared to support. In 1724 he rescinded William Wood's patent to mint copper coins for use in Ireland, because it aroused so much trouble for the Government that the successful management of affairs both in Ireland and at Westminster was put in jeopardy. In 1737 he agreed to water down the bill designed to punish the town council and citizens of Edinburgh for not preventing the Porteous Riot of the previous year. If he had persisted with his original intentions he would have alienated Scottish opinion when he needed the support of the Scots in both Houses of Parliament. On two celebrated occasions he actually abandoned policies he clearly believed in, because of the strength of opinion in the Commons. In 1733 he decided to abandon his excise scheme because of growing opposition, and in 1739 he submitted to pressure from the Commons and agreed to a war against Spain.

In these few instances Walpole actually retreated under pressure, but of course, he could never have retained the support of the King or the respect of the Commons if he had abandoned his policies at the first sign of serious opposition. Most of the time he carefully calculated what would be the best means of safeguarding the Hanoverian Settlement and the Whig supremacy. He invariably concluded that these objectives could only be obtained if he carried the majority of the political nation with him. He therefore strove to maintain domestic harmony and to pursue measures which would prove palatable to most Members of Parliament. This usually meant assessing how far he could push certain policies, when was the best time to intro-duce particular policies, or how he might make concessions to some powerful vested interests in order to secure their support for other measures which they might not otherwise have supported.

This shrewd assessment of what was politically feasible and this careful balancing of the main interests in Parliament can be illustrated by an examination of Walpole's religious policy. The Whigs, and particularly the more radical members, had long been attached to the cause of religious toleration. Most Dissenters had reciprocated by supporting the Whigs in parlia-mentary elections and in the Commons. Although relatively few in numbers, the Dissenters had considerable influence in the financial and merchant community in the City of London and, over the years, they had developed highly sophisticated political techniques in their efforts to exert maximum pressure on Gov-ment and Parliament. In response to the lobbying of the Dissenters and in order to satisfy the demands of many Whigs, Walpole was ready to relax the legal restrictions imposed on Protestant Nonconformists.

He was aware, however, that in obliging the Dissenters he could not afford to alienate the Anglicans. The Church of Eng-land was declining in authority and influence, and the high-churchmen were unable to arrest this trend because of the appointment of Whig bishops and the permanent prorogation of Convocation; but the majority in Parliament was still reluc-tant to see any attack on the special privileges of the Established Church. Walpole had learned in 1710 how powerful the Anglican interest could be, if it feared that the Church was in danger. He therefore realized that it would be impossible to satisfy the Dissenters and the radical Whigs to the extent of repealing the Test and Corporation Acts. Instead, from 1727 he began to pass annual Indemnity Acts, which did not remove these disabilities from the Dissenters, but which indemnified those who held office without taking the sacrament in the Church of England as laid down by the Test and Corporation Acts. His position in the Commons was too weak for him to pass these Acts in 1730 and 1732, but this did not prevent the Dissenters campaigning for greater concessions. They embarked on extensive lobbying campaigns, though Walpole was generally able to control their activities by pointing out how inopportune it was to make such demands in the present circumstances. When the Dissenters lost patience and pressed their own Members to introduce bills to repeal the Test and Corporation Acts, in 1736 and again in 1739, Walpole voted against them. This enabled him to pose as the defender of the privileges of the Church of England, while not risking the support of the Dissenters. They knew quite well that no politician could do any more for them than Walpole had attempted. This was confirmed when Walpole pushed a Tithe Bill, which aimed to free the Quakers from prosecutions in the church courts, through the Commons in 1736, only to see it thrown out by the Lords.

In marked contrast to Anne's reign, when religious issues had created major political crises, Walpole's years in power witnessed no serious disturbance over religion. He secured domestic harmony not by total inaction, but by acknowledging the superior strength of the church interest while protecting the Dissenters from the worst consequences of the laws against them. He gained valuable support without making too many enemies. He pursued the same tactics in the Government's two major areas of responsibility, financial and foreign affairs. In both spheres he pursued policies which were designed to safeguard the Hanoverian Settlement and the Whig supremacy, but which could be certain of securing the support of the majority in Parliament. Walpole's financial and foreign policies, however, are so important and so central to any understanding of his career and achievement, that they need to be considered at length in the next two chapters.

6   Financial and Commercial Policies

Walpole's careful calculation of the political consequences of his actions can be clearly seen in his financial and commercial policies. To remain in power he had to convince the King that he could persuade Parliament to vote the revenue needed by the Court and the Government. To persuade Parliament to vote the necessary supplies, he had to convince a majority of Members that he was competent to manage the nation's finances and capable of promoting the country's economic welfare. Walpole, however, was not just interested in power for its own sake. He had wider political aims – to unite the nation behind the Hanoverian Settlement and the Whig supremacy. He had personal experience of the bitterness and divisions which could be created by an unstable financial structure, heavy taxation, and the dislocation of economic life. These financial and economic strains, which had been so apparent in Anne's reign and during the crisis of the South Sea Bubble, had aggravated the political rivalry between Whigs and Tories, had intensified the social conflict between the landed and the moneyed interests, and had encouraged the enemies of the Hanoverian succession. Walpole hoped to reverse these unfortunate political developments and promote domestic harmony by his financial and commercial policies. His financial policies were designed to enable him to raise the revenue needed by the Government, to persuade the landed interest to consent to the necessary taxation, and to borrow the ready cash from the financial interest. His commercial and economic policies were designed to promote the prosperity of the country as a whole and to stabilize the nation's finances so that the landed, moneyed, and merchant interests, or at least large parts of them, would support his administration.

The first and most essential task of any ministry was to persuade the Commons to vote sufficient revenue to enable the Government to meet the financial burden of conducting the nation's affairs. No Government in the eighteenth century was expected to raise the vast sums needed by modern administrations to meet the cost of their national programmes of social and economic reforms. Nevertheless, Parliament was still expected to vote quite considerable sums of money to meet the expenses of the Court, the administrative departments, and the armed forces. After the Revolution Settlement more effective means of raising large-scale loans of ready cash from City financiers had depended on the ability of successive administrations to persuade the Commons to vote the revenue needed to pay the interest on this National Debt. Although the revenue had always been granted, the landed interest, which predominated in the Commons, had often complained about the high level of taxation and about the unequal burden imposed by the land tax. Because this new tax was easily assessed and collected, it became the favourite means of raising additional revenue. As a result, it was levied at the high rate of four shillings in the pound during the wars of William III and Queen Anne. The landowners had found it difficult to shift this burden of tax onto their tenants because the poor returns on farming during these years had not equipped these farmers with the financial resources to meet this additional burden. In consequence, the squirearchy eventually revolted. Their sense of grievance produced the Tory reaction of 1710 and the widespread demand for a speedy peace with France. Walpole was determined to avoid a similar reaction to his financial policies.

As the head of the Treasury and the principal minister in the Commons, Walpole alone bore the heavy responsibility of devising the means of raising the revenue needed by the Government. Although he deservedly won the reputation of being a first-class finance minister, he was not a great innovator. He stuck to the accepted methods of raising revenue, but he tried to ensure that his financial demands would arouse little resistance in the Commons. By avoiding any involvement in a major war until 1739, he was able to reduce the actual burden of taxation; and by devising other means of raising revenue, he was able to spread the burden of taxation to a wider section of the community. He deliberately aimed to reduce the land tax so that the backbench squires, who for so long had looked to the Tories to protect their interests, would abandon their objections to the Hanoverian Settlement and the Whig supremacy. From 1722 to 1726, in 1730, and again from 1733 to 1739, Walpole was able to keep the land tax down to two shillings in the pound. In 1731 and 1732 he even managed to reduce it to the very low level of one shilling in the pound. In 1728 and 1729 the threat of war forced the assessment up to three shillings; in 1727 and from 1740 the reality of war pushed the level up to four shillings in the pound. In order to keep the land tax at a satisfactory level during most of his administration, Walpole and his treasury advisers, William Lowndes and John Scrope, had to devise means of increasing the yield from indirect taxes. Though his main aim was to appease the landed interest, he argued that everyone should pay taxes, since everyone benefited from the stability and effectiveness of a Government properly supplied with revenue. Thus, in 1730, he had hoped that the Commons would prefer to repeal the duty on candles rather than the salt duty because the former hit the rich much harder than the poor. Two years later, when he restored the salt duty, he argued that it was one of the most equitable of taxes since virtually everyone contributed to it. He ignored the Opposition's justifiable claim that the poor had to spend a much greater proportion of their income to pay this duty. Walpole was less concerned with justice to the poor than with keeping the land tax at one shilling in the pound for another year.

The same desire to appease the landed interest led him to impose other indirect taxes on items of popular consumption, notably excise duties on malt and beer. It also encouraged him to replace import duties on some goods by excise duties, a decision which resulted in the only significant defeat he experi-

enced over his financial policies. Walpole believed that substantial revenue could be levied on such imported items of
consumption as tea, coffee, cocoa, wines, and tobacco. These
had once been luxury goods, but they were being increasingly
consumed by a wider section of the community. This rising
demand had encouraged a considerable amount of smuggling
and fraud in the operation of the customs regulations. Walpole
did not wish to curb the profitable trade in re-exporting these
colonial products to European markets, but he was anxious to
stop fraudulent practices and to prevent the loss of vital revenue
to the Exchequer. He therefore decided to abolish the old import and export duties on these goods, but to levy an inland
or excise duty when these goods were sold for domestic consumption. In order to enforce the collection of this revenue,
all imports of these products were to be lodged in bonded warehouses on their arrival in a British port. A small duty was then
levied on all these goods, but, if they were later re-exported,
no further duty was paid; whereas, if they were sold in Britain,
they were subject to an inland or excise duty. The Government's
revenue officers were then in a position to check whether
domestic retailers could prove that their goods came from a
bonded warehouse. If they could not supply such evidence they
were probably selling smuggled goods. Walpole first experi-
mented with this scheme in 1724, when he abolished the old
duties on tea, coffee, cocoa, and chocolate, replacing them
with heavy inland or excise duties. The experiment aroused
little opposition and proved a considerable success. Revenue
was increased by about £120,000 *per annum* and yet
the re-export trade in these colonial products continued to
expand.

The success of this scheme encouraged Walpole to propose in 1733 that it should be extended to cover wines and
tobacco. He evidently expected little resistance, but the Opposition was beginning to realize what a good case they could make
against taxes which were levied on items of popular consumption and which were collected or enforced by an army of excise
officers. They had seen how the excise on malt had provoked

riots in Glasgow in 1725 when Walpole had extended the duty
to Scotland, and they had evidence that the excise duty on all
compound spirits, imposed in 1729, was proving impossible to
collect. Considerable public hostility had also been aroused by
the vigilance of the excise officers, who were able to search
vessels and premises for articles which were subject to excise
duty. When Walpole decided to re-impose the salt duty in 1732,
the Opposition was able to test public opinion and to rehearse
all its arguments against excise duties. The debates in the Commons and in the press showed that any extension of the system
of bonded warehouses and excise duties would be bitterly
resented.

Walpole was not deterred, and in 1733 he proceeded to
introduce his proposal to levy an excise duty on tobacco. He
argued that his scheme would prevent smuggling and frauds,
would increase London's trade in the re-export of tobacco, and
would raise more revenue so that he would be able to keep the
land tax at one shilling in the pound, but he could not convince
the sceptics. In the press, in petitions from many trading constituencies, and in debates in the Commons, the Opposition
campaigned against the Excise Bill on both financial and political grounds. It was attacked not only because it increased
the tax burden on the poorer sections of society and was expected to lead towards further excise duties on items of popular
consumption, but because it gave revenue officers the right of
search when they suspected that goods which had not paid
the excise duty were being concealed. This was regarded as an
infringement of personal liberty and as a further step towards
an army of revenue officers, whose political activities would
increase the Crown's ability to subvert the independence of
the electorate and the Commons. Thus, Walpole's scheme was
depicted as a threat to the cherished liberties of Englishmen
and to the effective working of the balanced constitution.
Despite the exaggerated nature of these fears, Walpole was unable to stem the mounting clamour against the Tobacco Bill.
In April 1733 he decided to delay the next reading of this bill
so long that it could not be passed that session. He never even

introduced his bill to levy an excise duty on wine. Walpole remained convinced of the merits of his proposals, but political considerations forced him to amend his plans for raising revenue. He was compelled to increase the land tax, but only to two shillings in the pound because he resorted to other taxes which would not cause such widespread resistance. A large number of relatively light taxes were raised on such items of general use as malt, soap, candles, salt, and leather. This made the cost of collecting the revenue rather high in relation to the amount of money raised, though Walpole worked hard to reduce costs by maintaining a tight control over the system. By keeping the land tax low and by avoiding more excise duties on imported colonial produce, he could keep direct taxation at a low level and yet avoid stiff resistance to his indirect taxes.

Much of the revenue voted by the Commons was earmarked for the payment of the interest rates on the National Debt, a burden which alarmed the country gentlemen on the backbenches. Many of them did not fully understand the mysteries of Bank stock, exchequer bills, and irredeemable annuities, and they were jealous of the recent and rapid advancement of a powerful new interest based on something as insubstantial as paper funds and public credit. They did not appreciate the stability and value of a financial system which encouraged the public to supply the Government with large sums of ready cash in return for rates of interest guaranteed and paid by taxes voted by Parliament. What they concentrated upon was the huge debt which appeared to be beggaring the nation and the undue influence on the Government of a handful of upstart financiers of doubtful honesty. The financial strains and political tension created by the burden of shouldering the vast expense of the two recent wars against France and by the disaster of the South Sea Bubble confirmed all their worst fears. In order to restore their confidence in the financial system and retain their support for his administration, Walpole had to convince them that the financial revolution of the 1690s had not spawned an unmanageable monster which would inevitably ruin the nation. He achieved this by restoring financial stability after the

South Sea Bubble and by at least giving the impression that he had the National Debt under control. As we have seen, the finances of the South Sea Company were put on a sound footing by reducing the company's debt to the Exchequer, by persuading the Bank of England to buy up some of the company's holding of government annuities so that it was supplied with some ready cash, and by concentrating most of the company's activities in gilt-edged government stock. The investors who had unwisely converted their government annuities into South Sea stock in the summer of 1720 had to suffer a drastic cut in their income, though they received some compensation from the confiscated wealth of the company's fraudulent directors and from the proceeds of the surplus stock that had accrued to the company. For the rest of his years in power Walpole remained determined that the Government would never again default on its responsibilities to the public creditors. In achieving this aim, he restored the nation's confidence in the value of government annuities.

Despite the great, though temporary, shock to the system of public credit, the Government derived one permanent advantage from the South Sea Bubble. Since many holders of government annuities had exchanged them for South Sea stock, the Government had to pay lower interest rates on this portion of the National Debt. This, at least, gratified many of the independent country gentlemen. They were also encouraged to believe that the Sinking Fund, devised by Walpole though introduced by Stanhope in 1717, might eventually pay off the whole National Debt. For some years after the South Sea Bubble, Walpole kept the Sinking Fund operating in order to appease the fears of the majority in the Commons. Between 1717 and 1727, the surpluses from specific taxes were paid into the Sinking Fund and used to redeem over £6½ million of the National Debt. Thereafter, the surpluses accruing to the Sinking Fund continued to increase and, between 1727 and 1730, the rate of interest on government stock held by the Bank of England, the East India Company, and the South Sea Company was reduced from 5 per cent to 4 per cent so that the burden on the Exchequer was lighter than in 1721. This healthy state of affairs quieted the worst fears of the country gentlemen in the Commons, but there was never any chance that Walpole would be able to redeem the whole National Debt. During Walpole's twenty-one years in power he redeemed about £12½ million of the National Debt, but was forced to borrow just over £6½ million in new loans, so that the net decrease was a little more than £6 million. Moreover, he left the country involved in a major war which soon forced the Government to raise massive new loans.

Though his critics tried to belittle his achievement, it is clear that he did reduce the National Debt and restored the nation's confidence in the financial system. Nevertheless, it is also clear that he never expected the whole National Debt to be redeemed. He persevered with the Sinking Fund for political as much as for financial reasons. It was soon obvious that he could not find the surplus revenue to put into the Sinking Fund in those years when the threat of war forced the Government to find money for large armed forces. Any sudden increase in the demand for current expenditure always forced Walpole to raise fresh loans and to find the means of paying the interest on them. This could be easily done if he were prepared to take the political risk of continually raising the land tax. Because he wished to avoid irritating the independent country gentlemen in this manner, he preferred to ask them to let him raid the Sinking Fund. He thus deferred the plan to redeem the National Debt in order to avoid increasing the current level of taxation. At first, Walpole used the income of the Sinking Fund as security for new loans, but he eventually made more systematic raids on the fund. For example, the increased civil list for George II that was granted in 1727 was paid from the Sinking Fund; in 1729 the interest on a new loan of £1¼ million was met from the fund; and, from 1733, Walpole began to appropriate lump sums from the fund because the annual revenue was no longer sufficient to meet current expenses. By 1741 over £6½ million had been taken from the Sinking Fund to meet current expenses, and with the country involved in another major war in Europe, the last chance of redeeming the National Debt disappeared. By this time, however, Walpole had eased the fears of many back-benchers about the National Debt and he had encouraged financiers to continue to lend large sums of money to the Government at reasonable rates of interest. He had created a general atmosphere of financial confidence that enabled the more enterprising landowners to raise the money to improve their estates or invest in the mineral resources on their land. This climate also helped to promote the other financial services of the City of London in banking, fire insurance, and marine underwriting. The stability of the nation's finances reduced the tension between the landed and the moneyed interests, and encouraged the capital investments needed to stimulate the country's economy. These were major achievements after the bitterness and panic created by the bursting of the South Sea Bubble.

The stability of the country's finances depended upon the healthy state of Britain's commerce, for much of the Government's revenue was raised from customs and excise duties. Moreover, although the country's major industry was still agriculture, Britain's prosperity depended more and more on commercial enterprise. Not only merchants, but financiers, industrialists, landowners, and many of the labouring classes benefited from Britain's import and export trade. Any marked decline in the export of woollen cloth, for example, would have had serious repercussions throughout the whole economy. Walpole was therefore concerned to improve Britain's trading position in relation to her major competitors. To do so, he adopted a policy which was openly protectionist and restrictionist, like those practised by most contemporary European powers. A master of technical detail, Walpole drew up clear, practical, and direct plans to protect and foster British manufactures and to reduce the price of exported goods in an effort to increase their sales throughout the world. While he cannot really be regarded as an innovator or as a major reformer in economic affairs, Walpole did produce a coherent and consistent policy which was designed to increase employment and prosperity at home, and improve Britain's balance of trade with her European rivals. As early as 19 October 1721 Walpole laid down the guidelines of his economic policy in the King's Speech to both Houses of Parliament:

> It is very obvious that nothing would more conduce to the obtaining of so public a good, than to make the exportation of our own manufactures and the importation of the commodities used in the manufacturing of them, as practicable and as easy as may be; by this means, the balance of trade may be preserved in our favour, our navigation greatly increased and great numbers of our poor employed.

The customs duties raised on both imported and exported goods were very complicated, and sometimes as many as ten different duties were levied on the same article. Most duties were a proportion of the value of the article as laid down in the official Book of Rates, but often this bore no relation to the current value of the article and not all articles were listed. Walpole tried to overhaul the system in order to reduce both confusion and fraudulent practices. In 1723 the separate customs services of England and Scotland were brought under one commission. In 1724 a supplementary Book of Rates, which gave the official valuation of a large number of articles not in the old book, was published. Customs and excise officers were also instructed to make greater efforts to detect frauds and to curb smuggling. During Walpole's years in power hundreds of vessels were seized and thousands of individuals were prosecuted for evading the customs and excise regulations. The illicit trader might grumble at these developments, but many legitimate merchants found that they benefited from the speed and efficiency of their dealings with the improved customs and excise services.

Walpole's most significant reform was his decision in 1722 to abolish the export duties on nearly all articles manufactured in Britain in an effort to reduce their price on foreign markets. To further this end Walpole began abolishing or reducing the import duties on foreign raw materials needed in the production of British manufactured articles. This policy was applied in particular to Britain's greatest exports, namely textiles. The duties on a whole variety of imports needed for dyeing were reduced or abolished. Similar concessions were made on old rags and ropes used by paper manufacturers; on hemp and timber from the American colonies that were required by the ship-building industry; on flax needed by the linen industry; on beaver skins to be made into hats; on diamonds and precious stones used by jewellers; and on whale, seal, and fish products required by a variety of manufacturers. Other means were also found to promote domestic manufacturing industries. High duties were imposed on some foreign manufactured articles, such as linen and French silk. The import of some products, such as oriental silk cloth and painted calico, was prohibited alto-gether in an effort to protect British manufacturers from stiff foreign competition. To encourage the sale of some British pro-ducts abroad, including manufactured silk, sail-cloth, linen, re-fined sugar, and paper, the Government awarded financial bounties for their export. Domestic manufacturers were also assisted by the regulations which reserved some British primary materials for their exclusive benefit. Wool was the most im-portant of these. The laws against the export of wool were rigorously, although not always successfully, enforced. An ex-port duty was also levied on unfinished 'white' cloth in an attempt to encourage the dyeing and finishing of all woollen cloth in Britain. Two major primary products were exempt from these export regulations – coal and grain. These were vital for several industries; grain, for example, was used extensively in brewing. Walpole, however, was more concerned in these two instances to stimulate mining and agriculture, and to pro-vide the shipping industry with bulk freight.

Walpole tried to encourage British manufacturers by other regulations besides changes in import and export duties. A num-ber of restrictions were put on potential competitors in Ireland and the American colonies. The Irish linen industry was sabo-taged and the export of woollen cloth from Ireland to Europe was prohibited. In 1722 the Government decided that, because of their value to Britain's ship-building industry, no white pines in the American colonies should be felled or destroyed without a royal licence. In the same year copper and beaver skins were added to the list of enumerated products which the colonists could export only to England and which they could not use in their own industries. Ten years later the American colonies were forbidden to export hats or felts because they competed with British products.

Walpole also tried to protect British manufacturers from the demands of their workers. He reduced the costs of the employers and disciplined their labour force by legislation to keep wages low, to forbid workers combining to improve their conditions of employment, and to make it more difficult for unemployed men to obtain poor-relief. In 1721 the Government passed an Act to prevent London journeymen tailors from demanding higher wages. In 1726 complaints were made in the Commons against the violent efforts of weavers and other workers in the woollen industry to improve their wages and conditions. Walpole responded with an Act which punished such violence and which rendered illegal any contracts about prices, wages, or hours that had been demanded by combinations of workers. Legislation of this sort was not always successful and some workers still managed to unite in their efforts to improve their lot, but the passing of such Acts was symptomatic of Walpole's persistent efforts to promote the prosperity of British manufacturers and his lack of concern for the working conditions of the labouring classes.

Despite the determined efforts to improve Britain's trade and domestic industries, Walpole's success was limited. Commercial statistics for the years from 1721 to 1742 are by no means reliable, but they do indicate that the value of his reforms has usually been exaggerated. Trade was measured according to the value of the goods at their port of exit, so that the value of imports from other countries was often underestimated in the customs returns. Wars, storms, and smuggling all served to make the official figures an inaccurate guide to the value or volume of trade. No attempt was made at the time, and it is impossible now, to calculate accurately how much Britain benefited from her invisible earnings from banking, insurance, and shipping. Nevertheless, despite these reservations, the available evidence suggests that Walpole's policies did not have a major impact on Britain's trade and industries. The abolition of export duties had some beneficial effects, but there was no sharp rise in general exports after the reforms of 1722. The old duties had not been very high anyway, and so the slight reduction in the cost of British exports could not have much effect unless there were other reasons for an increased demand for them in foreign markets. Conversely, Walpole did not reduce the import duties on colonial products such as sugar, tobacco, rice, and coffee, and yet there was a great increase in the import of these products because of changing incomes and tastes in Britain and because of the reduction in the price of some of these products.

Walpole's tariff reforms therefore were inadequate while other adverse conditions persisted. Other colonial powers, notably the French, Dutch, and Spanish, brought colonial goods to Europe to compete with those from British territories. Transport costs, higher wage levels in Britain, and tariff walls in Europe all added to the price of British goods in these markets. Most countries in Europe practised the same protectionist policies as Walpole in an effort to stimulate their own domestic industries. Even the demand in Europe for Britain's greatest export, woollen cloth, decreased in this period. Bounties on exports and protective tariffs against foreign imports could not ensure the development of those British industries that produced goods for which there was not a heavy demand at home or abroad. Until prices could be significantly reduced and profit margins increased, by means of a substantial rise in demand and a vital reduction in costs due to improved techniques of mass production, there were no effective ways of promoting the sale of many British manufactured goods at home or in the markets of the world. The demand in some areas of Europe for British manufactured articles had temporarily reached saturation point. Thus, the volume of trade with Europe rose very slowly in comparison to the rapid increase in the later seventeenth century and again in the later eighteenth century. Trade with the West Indies and the American colonies, both in the import of raw

materials and the export of manufactured articles, did grow
rapidly but this improvement owed little to Walpole's reforms.
Moreover, it brought British merchants into competition with
the French and Spanish. By the mid-1730s many of the merchants engaged in the Atlantic trade believed that Walpole's
protectionist policies were not enough to promote Britain's overseas trade. They demanded a more aggressive policy and
eventually, in 1739, forced Walpole into declaring war against
Spain to protect Britain's trading interests.

Walpole's economic and commercial policies were too
limited in their nature and scope to have a profound effect. No
British Government of this period would have dared interfere
extensively in local and individual economic activities, and none
possessed the facilities, resources, or expertise to manage the
country's economy. Walpole's actions could only have a
marginal effect. They had virtually no effect on agriculture,
which was the most important sector of the economy. Throughout most of the 1730s there were good harvests, which meant
that the price of grain fell heavily. With reduced incomes many
tenant-farmers fell behind with their rents and some even
abandoned their farms, while the smaller landowners, the Tory
squirearchy, were faced with the prospect of tightening their
belts in the hope of better times or selling out. The greater landowners, the Whig oligarchs, survived without too much strain
because they had other sources of income, such as court
appointments, and could improve their estates in order to
increase the yield to make up for the fall in prices. The labouring
poor may have benefited marginally by the reduction in the
price of food. Walpole's economic reforms had little effect on
any of these developments. The Government's bounties on the
export of grain provided a minority of farmers and landowners
with a little extra income, but most agricultural produce was
sold on the domestic market. The country gentlemen gained
much more by Walpole's attempts to keep down the level of the
land tax and by the restoration of financial stability, which
made it easier for them to raise loans to improve their estates
or to tide them over the years of low grain prices.

Although the effect of Walpole's economic and commercial reforms has often been exaggerated, this does not mean that all his measures were unsuccessful or of little value. It is impossible to calculate the precise effect of his tariff reforms, but he deserves some credit for the commercial advances made while he was in power. The total value and volume of British trade certainly increased between 1721 and 1742. The value of exports probably rose by about one-third, while imports advanced by just over one-fifth. The balance of trade was healthier and the country was more prosperous. The increased trade, particularly in such bulk cargoes as sugar, tobacco, timber, coal, and grain, also stimulated the shipping industry and improved the facilities in many ports. Walpole's tariff reforms were only one of many reasons for the relative improvement of Britain's trading position. The effect of his protectionist policies, however, probably had a more significant impact on Britain's domestic industries. High tariff walls against the import of foreign manufactured articles helped promote greater industrial self-sufficiency. Certainly the silk and linen industries in Britain were slowly and painfully built up only because they were protected from stiff foreign competition by the kind of policies pursued, if not initiated, by Walpole.

The economic consequences of Walpole's financial and commercial policies may have been less significant than he hoped, but there can be no doubt about the political success of these policies. Walpole not only achieved his first aim, to raise the revenue needed by the Government without alienating the important social and economic interests in the community, but also succeeded in reconciling these powerful interests to the Hanoverian Settlement and the Whig supremacy. His financial and economic policies were designed with this political end clearly in view, and he was prepared to amend them if they aroused too much opposition. Everyone, including the financiers themselves, benefited from the restoration of financial stability and confidence. The landed interest was gratified by the attempts to pay off the National Debt and to keep the land tax as low as possible. Many merchants and manufacturers gained a measure of assistance from Walpole's tariff reforms and he abandoned his excise scheme of 1733 in the face of heavy criticism from the trading community. In general, however, it is clear that he concentrated on protecting the vested interests of the land-owners and of the established financial and commercial corporations of the City, for these groups were powerfully represented in Parliament. He was not so concerned to protect the interests of the less influential and less organized sections of the merchant community. His foreign policy, in particular, was designed to keep the peace in order to keep the land tax low and promote the trade of the great corporations. He was less willing to respond to the demands of the independent merchants engaged in the Atlantic trade who wanted to be protected from interference from the Spanish coastguards operating in West Indian waters. By the late 1730s, however, the hostility of these merchants caused him considerable trouble in Parliament and in many constituencies. In 1739 he bowed to this pressure and declared war on Spain.

Walpole developed very close working relations with the financial interest of the City of London. The political power of the City was exaggerated by the backbench squires. The financiers were not strong enough in Parliament to rival the influence of the landed interest and they could not afford to alienate the Government, since their fortunes depended on lend-ing money to the nation and having their financial and commercial privileges protected. Nevertheless, their support for Walpole's administration was a vital political asset. He needed their help in order to raise the frequent loans required by the Government, to reduce the rate of interest on the National Debt from 5 per cent to 4 per cent, and to restore financial con-fidence after the disaster of the South Sea Bubble. In return for this support, Walpole made sure that the financiers need never again fear for their investments or their privileges. In 1737 Sir John Barnard, a prominent Opposition spokesman, suggested to the Commons that the financial situation was now so good that the interest on the National Debt should be reduced yet again to a mere 3 per cent. This proposal, which would reduce the financial burden on the whole nation and probably lead to a cut in taxation, naturally attracted considerable support in the Commons even among the supporters of the ministry. Walpole, however, argued that it would be dangerous to create financial uncertainty when the Government was already working on a policy of redeeming the National Debt through the revenue in the Sinking Fund. He also claimed that any reduction in the rate of interest would hit thousands of small investors who depended upon their income from government annuities. While this was quite true, for more and more small investors had been attracted by the security of government funds, Walpole was really more concerned to protect the interests of the great City financiers.

Walpole's defeat of Barnard's scheme was a major service to the financial interest, but it was not the only effort he made to protect the great financiers and merchants of the City. The East India Company and the South Sea Company were heavy subscribers when the Government required large loans, but they were also concerned with the promotion of their overseas trade. Their financial and commercial interests put these two companies among the most powerful pressure groups in Parliament and so Walpole was anxious to secure their political support. In February 1730 Sir John Barnard and other Opposition leaders in the Commons encouraged petitions from a large number of merchants in London, Bristol, and Liverpool, who desired to put an end to the East India Company's trading monopoly with India and the East Indies. Walpole defeated this proposal and promptly renewed the company's charter until 1766. In return for this assistance the company paid the Government £200,000 and agreed to follow the Bank of England in accepting a reduction of the rate of interest on its government funds from 5 per cent to 4 per cent. Walpole was even more determined to protect the company from foreign competition and, in this endeavour, he had the support of the Opposition. Since 1718, merchants in the Austrian Netherlands had been engaged in competition with the English and Dutch East India companies. In 1722 the Emperor had granted a charter to the Ostend Company to regulate this trade with the east. This threat to British commercial interests stimulated Parliament into demanding action from the Government. By 1726 there was widespread support in the Commons for the suggestion that the Government should seek to destroy the Ostend Company. This encouraged Walpole and Townshend to put pressure on the Emperor. In 1727 the Emperor agreed to suspend the company's charters, and then he deserted its cause forever when he signed the second Treaty of Vienna in 1731.

The South Sea Company, although it was never such a great trading company as the East India Company, still expected the Government to protect its interests when they were threatened by the interference and restrictions of the Spanish authorities. Walpole was reluctant to support the company in its disputes with Spain over its commercial privileges, but the company was able to convince Newcastle and other ministers of the justice of its complaints against the King of Spain. The company's stubbornness frustrated Walpole's attempts to negotiate a satisfactory settlement of the disputes. When, however, the numerous other merchants engaged in the Atlantic and West Indian trade, whether legitimately with British colonies or illicitly with Spanish America, began to demand protection from the activities of the Spanish coastguards in the area, Walpole had to abandon any hope of a peaceful settlement. Public opinion was so incensed at Spain's interference with Britain's commercial interests that Walpole found it politically expedient to give way to the demands for an aggressive policy. In 1739 he was pushed into a war by the widespread demands that the Government should protect Britain's commercial interests.

Whenever the merchant community sought to protect its interests by exerting strong political pressure on the Government, it could expect Walpole to respond. The West India merchants, though they had not formed a great trading corporation, were numerically the strongest commercial pressure group in Parliament. Both the rich absentee proprietors of West Indian plantations and the London merchants actually engaged in the profitable trade were well represented in the Commons. By the 1730s the West India planters and merchants were concerned at the way the increasing demand for sugar, molasses, and rum in Britain, Ireland, and the American colonies was being met by the importation of these goods from the French West Indies, where they were produced more cheaply. This situation encouraged the West India interest to lobby the ministry and the Commons by means of petitions, pamphlets, and detailed information in order to secure some protection from this French competition. Walpole listened sympathetically to their case. In 1733 he passed the Molasses Act. This measure levied prohibitive duties on all foreign sugar, molasses, and rum imported into the American colonies and also cut the trade in these goods between the French West Indies and Ireland. In 1739 the Sugar Act allowed the export of West Indian sugar direct to southern Europe, though exports to northern Europe still had to be landed first at a British port. This privilege was not aimed at increasing exports to southern Europe, but at encouraging British importers to pay the higher price for sugar from the British West Indies or risk seeing it sold abroad instead.

The Russia Company could not match the political influence of the West India interest, but, compared to its main rival, the Levant Company, it had more support in Parliament and in the outports. It also had a more efficient organization and the added advantage that its governor was Samuel Holden, an influential director of the Bank of England, the leading spokesman for the Dissenting interest, and a personal friend of Walpole. When the company complained to Walpole that high tariffs and other restrictions imposed by the Tsar were obstructing its trade with Russia, the minister saw his opportunity of encouraging this trade while also securing closer diplomatic relations with Russia. From 1730 to 1734 the Government was involved in delicate negotiations with the Tsar, and throughout these years it received and acted upon the advice of the Russia Company. When the detailed and tedious negotiations were completed by the commercial treaty of 1734, the Russia Company secured all its principal objectives and its trade expanded rapidly. In 1741 the company was allowed to import raw silk from Persia via Russia, though this contravened the Navigation Act of 1660, which required that goods imported into Britain should come direct from their country of origin.

It is clear from these examples of Walpole's actions on behalf of powerful commercial interests that his economic strategy was not simply a policy of letting sleeping dogs lie. He was quite ready to interfere in commercial affairs if he could promote Britain's trading interests and secure political support for his administration. Before he acted, he carefully calculated the political advantages. Thus, he was prepared to face strong opposition in the American colonies to the Molasses Act because he secured the political support of the West India interest in the Commons and protected British commercial interests against French competition. He was not against helping the American colonies when this was feasible, for in 1730 he allowed Carolina to export rice direct to southern Europe and in 1738 he widened this breach in the Navigation Acts when he extended this privilege to Georgia. Walpole was also prepared to contravene the Navigation Acts and risk the hostility of the Levant Company in his efforts to assist the Russia Company, because he believed that the political, diplomatic, and commercial advantages outweighed these other considerations. When Walpole withdrew his cherished excise scheme in 1733 and abandoned his efforts to avoid war by engaging in hostilities against Spain, these were only the most important examples of his readiness to allow political considerations to dictate his commercial policies.

7 Foreign Policy

Walpole's grasp of financial matters was formidable and made him almost indispensable to the King. In the management of foreign policy, however, he was less accomplished. Despite occasional successes, he proved himself to be ill-equipped for the conduct of diplomacy and foreign affairs. While the legend that he conversed with George I in dog-Latin has been exploded, his knowledge of French, the diplomatic language of this period, was not extensive. He could probably read French, perhaps with the aid of a dictionary, but his ability to speak the language fluently must be seriously questioned. George I's own knowledge of French was not that much greater, so that in the early years of his reign he relied heavily on Robethon, the Hanoverian diplomat, to act as an interpreter during his private audiences with his English ministers. Walpole could certainly not converse in German, an accomplishment which endeared Carteret to the Hanoverians. Nor did Walpole have any first-hand experience of foreign affairs when he came to power in 1721. He had never travelled in Europe and none of the offices which he had held during his political career had been directly concerned with the conduct of foreign policy.

It did not take Walpole long to appreciate that he laboured under two major handicaps, at Court and in Parliament, because of his lack of knowledge and experience of foreign affairs. In the first place, his deficiencies weakened his influence at Court. Both George I and George II often appeared more concerned with the fate of Hanover than with the interests of Britain. They were certainly more interested in the affairs of Europe than in domestic politics. A minister who made no effort to share this concern and interest would not have carried much weight at Court. If he lacked knowledge and experience, he would not be able to advise his sovereign on the use of the Crown's most important prerogative, the formulation and execution of foreign policy. This would leave the King or those who did have his ear on such topics with too much freedom of manoeuvre for the peace of mind of a minister like Walpole, who desired to dominate all the Government's policies. By 1721 he had already experienced the power of a Secretary of State such as Stanhope, who had won the confidence of the King, and he soon discovered the threat to his influence posed by Carteret and even by his friend, Townshend. They often advocated action in Europe which pleased the King, but which created considerable political problems for Walpole at Westminster. Walpole therefore learned that if he were to have the greatest influence with the King, to dominate the counsels of the inner cabinet and to shape all the major policies of the administration, he had to take a much greater interest and a much greater role in the conduct of foreign affairs.

Walpole also realized that he needed to become more involved in foreign policy if he were to succeed in his aim of managing Parliament. In theory the conduct of foreign affairs remained the prerogative of the Crown, and Walpole was sometimes able to exploit this tradition to prevent the Opposition in the Commons inquiring too closely into the conduct of diplomacy during his administration. In the debates in 1730 on the fortifications of Dunkirk and in 1738–9 on the Spanish attacks on British ships, Walpole argued that the Commons could not expect to be shown the secret letters which had passed between George II and the courts of France and Spain. Nevertheless, Walpole realized that, in practice, no foreign policy could be conducted successfully without the consent of Parliament. Subsidy treaties, commercial treaties, and treaties ceding territories formally annexed to the Crown, all required parliamentary approval. The Act of Settlement of 1701 had also laid down that the Hanoverians must seek the agreement of Parliament before engaging in any war for the defence of Hanover.

Even more important was the inescapable fact that the maintenance of the army and the navy, whether in time of peace or war, was not possible without large supplies of money voted by the Commons. The conduct of diplomacy and war therefore became, with the voting of supplies, the most important topic debated by Parliament. As a result, the King's ministers had to spend much of their time in Parliament persuading the Members to support the Government's foreign policy. In the speech from the throne at the opening of every session the King mentioned foreign affairs, sometimes at great length. In virtually every session there were three or four major debates on foreign affairs, and in some years, 1729 to 1731 for example, this number was doubled. To win approval for their policies the ministers had to supply more and more information to Parliament to counter the Opposition's arguments. The great growth of the press at this time ensured that the Government's critics were not kept in ignorance about the affairs of Europe. Many London news-papers, particularly the great Opposition journals, received news from foreign embassies and from their own agents in Europe. William Pulteney was in direct contact with the Austrian ambassador, while Bolingbroke was on intimate terms with the French ambassador. When Spain announced in 1731 that she would no longer be bound by the terms of the Treaty of Seville, this embarrassing declaration, which threatened the recently cemented Anglo–Spanish agreement, first appeared in the English newspapers. Moreover, this news followed hard upon the revelation in *The Craftsman*, based on information received from the French ambassador, that Britain was planning to desert Spain and was already negotiating separately with the Emperor. This 'Hague Letter' and other Opposition news reports on the state of foreign affairs were reprinted in many provincial journals. In fact, foreign news was the most attractive feature to those who bought and read newspapers.

The Government therefore had to defend its foreign policy against informed criticisms. In the Commons this task fell upon Walpole, despite his lack of experience, because the Secretaries of State and all the other leading ministers sat in the Lords and because it was his duty as head of the Treasury to explain the ministry's request for votes of supply. To assist him he relied heavily on his brother, Horatio Walpole, who was more experienced and better informed, at least in the first few years of Walpole's administration. Though not a great speaker, Horatio was diligent and conscientious, and could be relied upon to give a straightforward explanation of the Government's policies. He also put in a lot of work with individual backbenchers in order to assess their reactions to particular controversial questions before the ministry committed itself publicly to a definite policy. Robert Walpole himself saw to it that informal statements or printed pamphlets, justifying the administration's actions, were widely circulated among the independent backbenchers. In 1726 a copy of the Treaty of Hanover, together with a statement of the Government's reasons for signing it, was distributed to every Member of Parliament. On other occasions, when the criticisms of the Opposition appeared to be swaying the independent backbenchers, Walpole replied by waging extensive propaganda campaigns. The Government's own newspapers, and individual pamphlets by writers such as Benjamin Hoadly and Horatio Walpole, defended and justified the ministry's policies. Robert Walpole contributed two such pamphlets in 1730: *Observations on the Treaty between the Crowns of Great Britain, France and Spain* and *The Treaty of Seville and the measures that have been taken for the last four years*. These contributions from his own pen show that Walpole was fully aware of the need to carry the independent backbenchers with him.

The political need to manage both King and Commons was not the only reason for Walpole's growing involvement in foreign affairs. He was also fully conscious of the danger that war could not only undermine his own power, but might destroy the Hanoverian Settlement and the whole political fabric of the nation. In his early career he had experienced the political tension and bitterness engendered by the heavy cost in men and money of a major conflict in Europe. The War of the Spanish Succession had shown Walpole how the country gentlemen in the Commons could be driven into opposition to the Government by heavy taxation and how the landed interest could grow to hate the moneyed men who supplied the Government with the steady flow of cash needed to keep large armies in the field. This friction had exacerbated the divisions between Whigs and Tories, and had driven many squires into an attitude of sullen resentment towards the Hanoverian succession and the Whig supremacy. Walpole's personal and political interests were bound up with the security of the Hanoverian Settlement and the Whig supremacy, and hence with his ability to reconcile the landed interest to the new political Establishment. He knew that success depended on reducing the land tax and the financial burden imposed by the National Debt. Neither of these aims could be achieved if the country was at war or had to be constantly in a state of readiness for war. Moreover, Walpole feared that war could destroy the existing political settlement by means of an invasion launched by a powerful foreign enemy or by a successful Jacobite rebellion. Walpole's fears may have been exaggerated, yet the war he tried hard to avoid, the War of the Austrian Succession, saw Britain suffer major defeats in the field, led to a sharp rise in the National Debt, and encouraged the Jacobites to embark on another rebellion. He was therefore determined to keep the country at peace.

This determination forced him to take a greater interest in Britain's foreign policy, even though at first he was reluctant to interfere in a field in which he lacked experience and in which he never became an expert. On 21 November 1739, after he had been forced into a war against Spain by the pressure from his colleagues and his opponents, he still defended his efforts to avoid such a conflict. He told the Commons:

I have lived long enough on the world to see the effects of war on this nation; I have seen how destructive the effects, even of a successful war, have been; and shall I, who have seen this, when I am admitted to the honour to bear a share in His Majesty's councils, advise him to enter upon a war while peace may be had? No, Sir, I am proud to own it, that I always have been, and always shall be, an advocate for peace.

During the first years of his administration Walpole did not take a very active role in the conduct of foreign policy. He was preoccupied with restoring financial stability after the South Sea Bubble, with his tariff reforms, with the Atterbury plot to restore the Pretender, and with other problems nearer home. His interest in foreign affairs was aroused by his rivalry with Carteret, one of the Secretaries of State, who hoped to become the King's favourite minister; but, in the actual handling of Britain's relations with Europe, Walpole preferred to rely on the greater knowledge and experience of his long-standing friend and brother-in-law, Viscount Townshend, and of his brother, Horatio Walpole, who was appointed Britain's ambassador to France. Until he had learned more about the diplomatic scene in Europe, Walpole was wise not to interfere with the policies of his ministerial colleagues. The relations between the major European powers were incredibly complicated and had not been settled by the series of treaties at the end of the War of the Spanish Succession.

By the end of this war both Britain and France were desperate for a respite after the long years of expensive campaigning. They were ready, at least for the time being, to sink their differences. France had been exhausted by her exertions in the recent fighting, had suffered some humiliating defeats, and had temporarily lost the hegemony of western Europe. The royal finances, the country's economy, and the French armed forces all needed a breathing-space to recover their strength. France's ambitions in Europe were also temporarily inhibited by the death of Louis XIV in 1715 and the succession of a sickly five-year-old child, Louis XV, who required the services of a regent, the Duke of Orleans. The Regent hoped that he might yet succeed to the throne. He therefore desired peace in Europe and the friendship of Britain in case of the sudden death of Louis XV. Britain, for her part, was just as ready to keep the peace. She had made substantial gains by the terms of the Treaty of Utrecht, and her commercial ambitions, at the expense of Spain and France, were temporarily assuaged. Her ministers were primarily concerned to secure the Hanoverian succession and the Whig supremacy against any Jacobite threat. They had no desire to create enemies abroad who might assist the Pretender. Her new King, George I, was more interested in protecting and extending the territory of Hanover than in Britain's commercial rivalry with France and Spain. His eyes were turned to the Baltic and northern Germany, and his fears were focused on Russia, Sweden, and Prussia. With such preoccupations, both George I and his Whig ministers desired peace with France and Spain. The Dutch too, Britain's staunchest ally in the last two wars, were anxious for peace. They had suffered more than any other power involved in these wars and they dreaded the effects of another major conflict on their trade and their economic prosperity. Although they believed that Britain had betrayed them during the negotiations leading to the Treaty of Utrecht, the Dutch could not afford to renounce her friendship or to seek redress by embarking on another war against France.

Unfortunately for the peace of Europe, the two other major combatants in the War of the Spanish Succession, Spain and the Empire, were not prepared to abide by the terms which had brought the fighting to an end. Spain had probably been strengthened by the loss of some of her outlying territory in Europe, but she was not reconciled to the loss of Gibraltar and she resented the commercial concessions she had been forced to make to Britain, especially when British merchants went beyond the terms of these concessions and engaged in illicit trade with Spanish America. Instead of concentrating on these issues, Spain weakened her position by becoming embroiled with the Austrians in northern Italy. The Queen of Spain, Elizabeth Farnese, who dominated her weak and neurotic husband, Philip V, was determined to secure for her sons the thrones of Parma and Tuscany, where she had quite strong claims to the succession. This brought her into conflict with the Emperor, for the Austrians were now the dominant force in northern Italy. If this had been the Emperor's only problem, he might have faced the threat with equanimity. He too, however, had not accepted the results of the recent fighting and he still laid claim to the whole Spanish inheritance for which he had once fought.

There was no real chance that he would ever be able to sit on the throne of Spain, especially as he laboured under several disadvantages. The Emperor ruled a heterogeneous collection of territories which were impossible to unite and whose defence requirements over-extended his power. Only his Austrian territories were secure. In the east he was in conflict with the Ottoman Turk; in the south he was threatened by Spain's ambitions in Italy; in the west his new possessions in the Netherlands excited the commercial jealousy of British and Dutch merchants; while in the north, despite his title of Emperor, he could not command the undivided allegiance of the German princes. To complicate matters further, he had no male heir and his room for diplomatic manoeuvre was continually restricted by his desire to persuade the governments of Europe to accept the Pragmatic Sanction, by which he hoped to secure the succession of his daughter, Maria Theresa, to all his territories.

When Walpole came to power in 1721 the situation was substantially the same as in 1715, but he still did not have a complete grasp of the intricacies of the diplomatic situation in Europe and so he was in no position to offer expert advice to George I or to the two Secretaries of State, Carteret and Townshend. Nevertheless, he was not without opinions on what was in Britain's best interests in the conduct of foreign affairs. Peace in Europe would help him to stabilize the country's finances, to secure widespread support for the Hanoverian Settlement, and to thwart the designs of the Jacobites. To secure peace, he maintained that Britain must retain the friendship of France and must seek by diplomatic means to settle the outstanding disputes between the Baltic powers and between Spain and the Emperor. These objectives were easy to formulate, but extraordinarily difficult to accomplish, and so Walpole decided to trust Townshend's judgement. He was even reluctant to speak on foreign affairs in the Commons during his first years in power because he did not feel competent to explain the tangled web of European diplomacy. It did not take him long to realize, however, that he could not stand aside while his ministerial colleagues advised the King on the foreign policy which Britain should pursue and left him to persuade the Commons to foot the bill. In the summer of 1723 George I and both the Secretaries of State, who were with him in Germany, feared for the interests of Hanover because of Russia's aggressive intentions in the Baltic. They urged upon Walpole the need to send cash to persuade other powers in the area, including Denmark, to support Sweden's resistance to the ambitions of Peter the Great. Walpole could not openly reject their demand, but in a private letter to Townshend he expressed strong misgivings about this expensive way of winning friends in the Baltic and warned him that he could not guarantee that Parliament would vote the necessary supplies. He advised against any hasty action, so that if war did break out he would be able to convince the Commons that the conflict had not been precipitated by the ministry. This was shrewd advice, for the Russian threat did not in fact materialize and Hanover's position was strengthened by an alliance with Prussia that was secured by the Treaty of Charlottenberg.

Meanwhile, Walpole supported the diplomatic initiatives made by the British and French ministers to settle the outstanding disputes between Spain and the Empire. Although a congress was convened at Cambrai in 1722, it failed to produce any agreement even after years of discussion. In fact, both Spain and the Emperor grew to resent the pressure being put on them by Britain and France. Spanish pride was outraged with France in particular when the Spanish Infanta, who was betrothed to Louis XV, was returned to her parents. At the same time the Emperor was coming into conflict with Britain's commercial ambitions because of his support of the Ostend East India Company in the Austrian Netherlands. Their irritation with France and Britain drove the two rival powers together, at least temporarily. By sudden and direct negotiations Spain and the Empire appeared to have settled their old disputes. It was even rumoured that they had concluded a military alliance by the first Treaty of Vienna of 30 April – 1 May 1725. In retrospect it is clear that there was little chance of this agreement lasting. It might also appear odd that Britain and France should have been worried by this *rapprochement*, which they had themselves been trying to promote. They were alarmed, however, at the extent of the concessions made by Spain and they were worried at the prospect of an Austro–Spanish military alliance. Their fears led them to cement an alliance to combat a resurgence of the Empire. By September 1725 Britain, France, Hanover, and Prussia had concluded a defensive alliance by the Treaty of Hanover. Within a year Prussia had changed sides, but, meanwhile, first the Dutch and then the Swedes and the Danes had been persuaded to join this alliance.

These negotiations were the work of Townshend. Having helped Walpole to remove Carteret as the other Secretary of State in 1724, he dominated the ministry's foreign policy. While he positively relished the dramatic diplomatic situation created by the Treaty of Vienna, Townshend knew that this treaty posed several immediate threats to British interests because of the major concessions granted by Spain to the Emperor. Spain had allowed the Emperor's subjects to trade with her colonies on very favourable terms, which made the Ostend East India Company a serious rival to the English company engaged in this trade. The Emperor, encouraged by this treaty, seemed prepared once more to challenge the religious independence of the Protestant princes of north Germany, including Hanover. Townshend also feared that Spain might make another attempt to recover Gibraltar and he did not rule out the possibility of some Austrian or Spanish support for a Jacobite conspiracy. Walpole had accepted Townshend's arguments that Britain's interests required her to negotiate defensive alliances in response to the Treaty of Vienna and that Parliament must be persuaded to face the possibility of war in the near future. He even brought Horatio Walpole over from Paris to defend Townshend's policies in the Commons at the beginning of the new session in 1726. Nevertheless, despite this measure of agreement with Townshend and the ready acceptance of the Treaty of Hanover by Parliament, Walpole began to have reservations about the nature and extent of Townshend's reaction to the Treaty of Vienna.

The Secretary of State was not only worried about the

immediate threat to British interests, but was convinced that the Emperor was now powerful enough to act as the arbiter of Europe. He also feared that there was a secret marriage alliance which would unite Don Carlos of Spain with Maria Theresa and so re-create the huge empire of Charles V. Since Don Carlos also had a claim to the throne of France, Townshend was able to conjure up terrible prospects for the balance of power in Europe. These fears, which Walpole did not share and which in fact proved unfounded, drove Townshend towards policies that showed a marked hostility to the Emperor. He suggested that the royal navy should blockade the port of Ostend in order to interrupt the trade of the East India Company based there. Townshend also pressed Walpole for subsidies to persuade other powers to join the Hanover alliance. In this way he persuaded the Swedes and the Danes to sign. He had even more ambitious plans to win over the Turks and the Poles, though these were never realized. Walpole became alarmed at the cost of such a policy. Having persuaded Parliament to accept the Treaty of Hanover, and having excited fears about the threat posed by the Emperor to British interests, he had no alternative but to support many of Townshend's suggestions. He therefore persuaded the Commons to vote the necessary supplies to buy the support or neutrality of the German princes and to hire 12,000 Hessian troops in order to bring the strength of the army up to 26,000 men.

The confederation built up by Townshend was enough to deter the Emperor from any aggressive act. To this extent, his policy was successful. The cost of it, however, was so prohibitive that it disturbed Walpole. He realized that he had provided the reviving Opposition in Parliament with a powerful weapon with which to attack the policies of the Government. The decision to hire Hessian mercenaries and to increase the size of the army in peacetime were bound to arouse the prejudices of the independent backbenchers and to make the voting of supplies more difficult. The Opposition claimed that Parliament was being asked to vote a land tax of four shillings in the pound in order to protect the interests of Hanover. Walpole was always concerned about the opinions of the independent backbenchers, but he was not just worried about the parliamentary reaction to Townshend's policies. He himself believed that his colleague was exaggerating the extent of the threat posed by the Emperor, and he disliked Townshend's attempt to reverse Britain's traditional alliance with the Austrians.

In Walpole's eyes Spain was the chief threat to Britain's commercial interests because of her refusal to implement her earlier concessions to the South Sea Company and her opposition to the increasing volume of illicit trade with her American territories. His views were reinforced by the criticisms of Townshend's policies in Parliament and by the temporary outbreak of hostilities with Spain, in 1726–7, when Spain attempted unsuccessfully to regain Gibraltar. Spain soon lost her nerve for a major conflict with Britain, particularly when the Emperor failed to support her, and so a settlement was hastily patched up. Despite this short-lived war, Townshend still favoured coming to terms with Spain in order to isolate the Emperor; but Walpole was becoming convinced that the reverse of this policy would be more in Britain's interests. In this first serious disagreement between the two ministers Townshend prevailed, and Walpole bowed to his colleague's wider experience of European affairs and greater grasp of the niceties of diplomacy. The relations between them, however, were beginning to show signs of strain. Walpole, for the first time, openly questioned Townshend's right to conduct foreign policy without seriously considering the impact of his actions on Parliament, while Townshend believed that Walpole was seeking to dominate all the Government's policies and to subordinate all his ministerial colleagues to his own will. Other factors combined to widen the breach. In 1726 Townshend's wife, Dolly, the sister of Walpole, died, and her passing weakened the close personal relationship between the two ministers. After the accession of George II in 1727, Walpole found that he had greater influence at Court than Townshend and so he could risk losing his political support which had been so valuable while George I was alive.

From 1727 to 1729 Townshend tried to stifle Walpole's criticisms by settling Britain's disputes with Spain, while still pursuing his plans to isolate the Emperor. Walpole was not entirely happy with this policy, but at least it afforded the prospect of peace with Spain and it seemed likely to preserve Britain's close relations with the French, who were pursuing similar policies towards Spain and the Empire. In fact, because of his anxiety to retain the friendship of France, Walpole failed to appreciate how far the aims of France were gradually diverging from those of Britain. He listened too much to the advice of his brother, Horatio, who was attending the congress at Soissons that was trying to settle the disputes with Spain. Horatio Walpole, while serving as ambassador to France, had established friendly relations with Fleury, the chief minister of Louis XV, and had come to place complete confidence in him. For the next decade Fleury convinced the Walpole brothers that he desired to be on the best of terms with Britain and that he would follow their diplomatic initiatives to settle the problems of Europe. Whenever there seemed to be any disagreement or divergence of opinion between the two countries, Fleury put the blame on Chauvelin, the ambitious French foreign minister. The Walpoles were taken in by his subtlety and his servile manner, little appreciating the ruthless, vindictive streak in Fleury. They feared Chauvelin's determined pursuit of clearly defined French aims, but they failed to realize that Fleury desired the same ends, even if he was prepared to use more devious means and opportunistic tactics.

Robert Walpole was so anxious to retain the alliance with France that he was unable to recognize that it had always been based on expediency and the temporary convenience of the two countries, and not on any real or long-term identity of interests. Once France was safe from any disputes about the succession to Louis XV, and this was eased by the birth of the Dauphin in 1729, and once she had recovered from the ravages of the War of the Spanish Succession, it was inevitable that her desire to dominate western Europe, and her colonial and commercial ambitions overseas, would bring her into conflict with British interests. Fleury recognized this much more clearly than Walpole. For his part, Townshend was far too preoccupied with the serious threat which he believed was posed by the ambitions of the Emperor.

The misjudgement of Fleury by the Walpole brothers did not become apparent for some years, and the differences of opinion between Robert Walpole and Townshend did not prevent a measure of agreement between them on settling Britain's disputes with Spain. Negotiations with Spain became profitable once she discovered that her alliance with the Emperor was built on sand and that her natural ally was France. Spain was incensed when, in 1729, the Emperor first repudiated the idea of a marriage alliance between Don Carlos and his daughter, Maria Theresa, and then refused to allow Spanish garrisons into Parma and Piacenza. These rebuffs persuaded Spain to come to terms with Britain. Fleury encouraged this *rapprochement* because, now that the succession was secure in France, he hoped to restore the Bourbon alliance with Spain and planned to isolate the Emperor. When Spain and Britain began to negotiate, Fleury acted more as a mediator than as the ally of Britain. Walpole wanted an agreement with Spain, but he did not support Fleury and Townshend in their desire to isolate the Emperor, especially as Townshend proposed to implement this policy by further expensive subsidy treaties to bribe a number of German princes to desert the Emperor. Horatio Walpole and the Duke of Newcastle, the other secretary of state, favoured Robert Walpole's cautious approach and opposed Townshend's hasty, risky, and expensive diplomacy in Germany. Moreover, George II was becoming alarmed at the prospect of a military conflict with the Emperor and he began to criticize the bullying tone of Townshend's diplomacy.

Townshend's isolated position gave Walpole the chance to outmanoeuvre him. While Townshend was in Hanover, during the summer of 1729, Walpole reached an agreement with the other leading ministers on how to proceed with the negotiations with Spain. Newcastle, as Secretary of State for the Southern Department, was officially responsible for the conduct of relations with Spain. With the approval of George II and Queen Caroline, but without the acquiescence of Townshend, he sent William Stanhope to Spain to conclude the peace negotiations. The Treaty of Seville, signed in November 1729, arranged that the commercial disputes between Britain and Spain should be settled by commissioners appointed by both countries. It also committed Britain and France to the support of the Spanish claim that Parma and Piacenza should be garrisoned by Spanish troops. Walpole was delighted with this diplomatic triumph and celebrated it in a short pamphlet, *Observations upon the Treaty between the Crowns of Great Britain, France and Spain.* He at once planned to reduce the size of the armed forces and lighten the tax burden so that he could undermine the Opposition's recent campaigns in Parliament.

Walpole was immensely encouraged by the quick and easy diplomatic success which he had managed to achieve without the advice and support of Townshend. His first real experience of diplomacy convinced him that he no longer had to rely so heavily on the strongly independent mind of his brother-in-law. He believed that he could now afford to rely on his own judgement, and on the opinions and experience of his more cautious and amenable allies, Newcastle and Horatio Walpole. Townshend soon recognized that his control of foreign policy was being seriously challenged for the first time since the defeat of Carteret in 1724. He still hoped that events would justify his hostility towards the Emperor, but, when it became increasingly clear that British and Hanoverian interests were not being seriously threatened by the Emperor, his authority was undermined. Rather than accept a subordinate role to Walpole and Newcastle, he chose to resign in May 1730 and to devote his energies to the improvement of his estates in Norfolk. His place as Secretary of State was filled by the more amenable and complaisant William Stanhope, who had been elevated to the peerage as Lord Harrington for his services in negotiating the Treaty of Seville.

With Townshend out of the way, Walpole was in a strong position to shape the Government's foreign policy. Newcastle and Harrington were experienced in diplomacy, but they both lacked the courage and political authority needed to pursue the kind of risky and independent policies that Townshend had championed. They could offer advice, which was often sensible and usually cautious, but not for many years did they openly disagree with Robert Walpole. It was the same story with the professional diplomats; men such as Horatio Walpole, who went to serve at The Hague in 1734, Lord Waldegrave, the new ambassador to France, and Thomas Robinson, who was sent to the Imperial court at Vienna. They all had considerable experience and expertise, but none of them could challenge Robert Walpole's authority and all of them were willing to let him dictate the Government's foreign policy. Carteret, who had been ousted as Secretary of State in 1724, might have hoped to stage a political comeback now that Townshend had retired; but Walpole put an end to his hopes by persuading George II to dismiss him from his post as Lord Lieutenant of Ireland. Walpole was now left with almost a free hand in the conduct of foreign policy. Even though his experience was negligible, his success with the Treaty of Seville convinced him that he had no need to worry about his new responsibilities. Not until his mistakes and errors of judgement became apparent in the later 1730s did he cease to dominate Britain's foreign policy in the same manner as he controlled her domestic policies.

It can be argued that Walpole's foreign policy was more successful and better designed to serve Britain's interests than the policies advocated by Townshend. Certainly he avoided a major war for ten years and, in the meantime, he ensured that Britain would be more able, financially and economically, to bear the strains of war when she finally decided she would have to fight to protect her interests. It can also be maintained that when war with Spain and France eventually broke out, Walpole was in no position to avoid these conflicts. Nevertheless, it is also apparent that Walpole's foreign policy is open to serious criticisms. He was too preoccupied with the immediate problem of avoiding war to give adequate consideration to the long-term consequences of his actions. He knew that peace meant reduced taxes and therefore greater political support for his administration, the Hanoverian Settlement, and the Whig supremacy. What he did not fully appreciate was that peace could not be safeguarded by a government which never showed any willingness to fight. A policy of peace at almost any price only encouraged other powers, particularly France and Spain, to pursue their own selfish ambitions without fearing stiff resistance from Britain. If he had shown, much earlier, any disposition to fight, then Walpole might have avoided a war with Spain in 1739.

Another weakness in Walpole's conduct of foreign affairs was his confidence that even the most intractable problems in Europe could be resolved by diplomatic negotiations. He believed that because peace was in Britain's best interests then it must be to the advantage of all the powers in Europe to avoid war. Walpole was delighted with the Treaty of Seville, for example, but he failed to recognize that, while it revealed the good intentions of Britain, France, and Spain, it had in fact settled nothing. It had not persuaded the Emperor to accept Spanish troops in Italy, it had not settled but only postponed the commercial disputes between Britain and Spain, and it had not even touched upon such problems as the possession of Gibraltar. Walpole was blind, or shut his eyes, to the unpleasant facts that Britain's commercial interests clashed with those of Spain and France, and that both these Bourbon powers wished to curb the power of the Emperor. His policy of seeking the friendship of France, Spain, and the Empire was successful in the short term, but, in the long run, he had no chance of avoiding a conflict of interests between the four great powers of Europe.

For several years, however, Walpole's diplomacy appeared to be crowned with success. Having apparently settled Britain's disputes with Spain by the Treaty of Seville, he proceeded to reverse Townshend's policy of coercing the Emperor. When Spain and France suggested that military pressure should be brought to bear on the Emperor to force him to accept Spanish troops in the two Italian duchies, Walpole regarded this proposal as departing too far from the traditional support of the

Whigs for the Empire. Far from supporting his more aggressive allies, Walpole preferred to defy the terms of the Treaty of Hanover and to ignore the advice of his brother, Horatio, by opening secret negotiations with the Emperor. These negotiations rapidly culminated, in March 1731, in the second Treaty of Vienna. By the terms of this treaty the Emperor agreed to allow Spanish troops into the two Italian duchies and to rescind the charter to the Ostend East India Company. In return for these major concessions to Spain and Britain, the Emperor secured British support for the Pragmatic Sanction, recognizing the succession of Maria Theresa to all the Habsburg territories. This treaty, which solved some of the long-standing disputes between the great European powers, appeared to be another diplomatic triumph for Walpole. It reduced the degree of conflict between Spain and the Empire, it destroyed a threat to British commercial interests, and it restored the traditional friendly relations between Britain and the Empire. In addition, it enabled Walpole to reduce the size of the armed forces and the level of taxation, and to undermine the Opposition's main arguments that he was neglecting Britain's commercial interests and meekly following the dictates of the French Government.

Walpole therefore had good reason to congratulate himself on his diplomatic triumph, though he was not yet aware of the full import of his agreement with the Emperor. He mistakenly believed that he could reconcile France to the results of his secret negotiations by pointing out that he had persuaded the Emperor to accept one of the important terms agreed by Britain, France, and Spain at the Treaty of Seville. He also expected France to be pleased at the destruction of a rival commercial company in the Austrian Netherlands. Thus, France derived the same two advantages from the second Treaty of Vienna as Britain, without having to accept the Pragmatic Sanction. What Walpole failed to appreciate was that France opposed any policy which might strengthen the Habsburgs. Fleury feared that Maria Theresa would marry the Duke of Lorraine and extend Habsburg territory right up to France's eastern frontier. In that case the Habsburgs would be in a position to invade the heart of France from either Lorraine or the Netherlands. Far from seeking an agreement with the Emperor, it was in France's interests to seek the break-up of the widespread, heterogeneous Habsburg territories. She had no wish to see the integrity of these possessions guaranteed by the general acceptance of the Pragmatic Sanction, but, because of the second Treaty of Vienna, France would have to contemplate war with Britain if she later chose to reject the Pragmatic Sanction.

Fleury was therefore furious at the consequences of Walpole's secret negotiations and a distinct coolness crept into the alliance between France and Britain. This led directly to closer relations between France and Spain, resulting in the Family Compact between these two Bourbon powers, and to a clash between France and the Emperor in the War of the Polish Succession. While, from Britain's point of view, these were disastrous developments and they followed directly from the second Treaty of Vienna, they were not entirely the consequences of Walpole's diplomacy. It could be argued, with considerable justification that it was inevitable that France and Spain would revive the Bourbon alliance, that the conflicting interests of France and the Emperor would eventually result in war, and that the alliance between Britain and France would break down. The friendship between Britain and France had been based on the temporary needs of both countries for a period of peace to allow them to recover from their exertions in the last war and to settle their uncertain dynastic problems. By 1731 these aims had been achieved, while grounds for dispute were multiplying apace. Britain protested about the rebuilding of Dunkirk, France resented the commercial privileges Britain had wrung out of Spain, and both countries were involved in a number of commercial and colonial confrontations throughout the world. If war with France was all but inevitable, then Walpole was amply justified in repairing the old alliance with the Emperor, for Britain would need the assistance of a major power in Europe to combat the military superiority of France. Walpole, however, does not deserve the credit for such foresight. He had no desire to end the alliance with France and did not foresee war between the two countries. He had signed the second Treaty of Vienna because he thought it would solve the problems of Europe and preserve his majority in the Commons. It proved a short-sighted policy.

After 1731 the relations between Britain and France became increasingly strained. France succeeded in cementing a closer alliance with Spain in 1733, intrigued with Sweden and Denmark to detach them from their alliance with Britain, and even encouraged the parliamentary Opposition in Britain. Walpole persisted in believing that Fleury still desired Britain's friendship and that these policies were instigated by Chauvelin, even though there were indications that Fleury agreed with Chauvelin's policies. He certainly pursued the same objectives after the fall of Chauvelin in 1737. Because of his trust in Fleury and his overriding desire for peace, Walpole was unprepared for the Family Compact of 1733 and for the joint Franco–Spanish attack on Habsburg territories that same year. In February 1733 Augustus II, the King of Poland, died. Since the Polish monarchy was elective and the great powers desired a creature of their own choice on the throne, there was the usual disputed succession. The Emperor and Russia wished to have the son of Augustus elected, but France supported the candidature of Louis XV's father-in-law, Stanislaus Leszczynski, who had been deposed as King of Poland some years earlier. Walpole had no great interest in who was elected. His great concern was to avoid being dragged into war because of Britain's treaty obligations to both France and the Emperor. A war in Poland did not involve British interests, but if, as appeared likely, France attacked the Emperor in Germany, and Spain invaded his territories in Italy, then Britain might be called upon to fulfil her obligations under the second Treaty of Vienna to defend the integrity of the Habsburg territories.

Walpole, who was preoccupied by the opposition to his excise scheme and by his plans for the forthcoming general election of 1734, was determined to avoid war at all costs. George II and Queen Caroline, and most of the cabinet, including the two Secretaries of State, Newcastle and Harrington, were more fearful of a radical shift in the balance of power in Europe if France and Spain inflicted heavy defeats on the Emperor. George and Caroline also believed that it was the duty of Hanover to serve the Emperor when he was attacked by a non-German power, and they were encouraged to act upon this belief by Hatorff, their Hanoverian minister at St James's. Walpole countered this advice by a single-minded campaign to keep Britain out of the war. By bullying his cabinet colleagues and by months of patient argument at Court, he was able to prevent any decision to reject his declared policy of neutrality. He was assisted by the determination of Britain's traditional ally, the Dutch, to avoid becoming embroiled in this war and by Fleury's claim that France had been forced into the war by the aggressive actions of the Russians, who had driven Stanislaus off the Polish throne as soon as he had been elected to it. Walpole readily accepted this flimsy excuse even though France abandoned any hope of restoring Stanislaus to his throne and concentrated on attacking the Emperor in Germany.

French troops invaded Lorraine and besieged the Austrian strongholds on the Rhine, while Spain and Sardinia attacked the Austrians in northern Italy. Walpole replied by sending his brother, Horatio, to The Hague to consult the Dutch authorities and by feebly threatening military or naval action on behalf of the Emperor, though he had no intention of carrying out these threats. While he was indicating to the French that he might just possibly intervene in the war, he was warning the Emperor not to expect Britain's support against France. Throughout the war he was taken in by Fleury's assertions that he had not wanted this conflict and by his oft-proclaimed desire for Britain's mediation to bring about a speedy peace. While Walpole swallowed the bait and his brother conducted prolonged and fruitless negotiations at The Hague, Fleury was allowed a free hand to deal with the Emperor.

Walpole was outwitted and outmanoeuvred by Fleury, who negotiated directly with the Emperor and ignored Britain's attempts at mediation. The War of the Polish Succession had gone very badly for the Austrian armies, but the terms offered by France in 1735 were not too harsh. The Emperor was asked to cede Lorraine to Stanislaus, the defeated candidate for the Polish throne, with the reversion in favour of Louis XV of France after the death of Stanislaus. The Emperor was also asked to accept the loss of Naples and Sicily to Spain. In return, France was prepared to guarantee the Pragmatic Sanction, and Spain at last gave up her rights to Parma and Piacenza in northern Italy. Walpole and his colleagues tried to claim some credit for these moderate terms. They claimed that these terms would settle the succession to both the Polish throne and the Habsburg territories, and they maintained that the Emperor's power was no weaker than before. He had lost some indefensible territory, far from Vienna, but had strengthened his position in northern Italy. Walpole also derived considerable satisfaction from the domestic consequences of his policy of neutrality. He could point to his victory in the general election of 1734, and he could boast to Queen Caroline, 'Madam, there are fifty thousand men slain this year in Europe, and not one Englishman.'

Although Walpole reaped some political benefits in Britain, his policy of neutrality in the War of the Polish Succession is open to serious criticism. His weak and indecisive diplomatic initiatives had proved completely ineffective and he gave France and Spain the firm impression that he would not fight to protect the Emperor's interests. He also sacrificed Britain's honour and national interest by not supporting the Emperor. Walpole had been prepared to accept the French argument that technically the Emperor was the aggressor because of his hostility to Stanislaus and his preparations for war. Yet the Austrian troops had never invaded Poland, whereas French and Spanish armies had attacked Habsburg territories. Britain had therefore stood back while the Bourbon powers achieved a distinct shift in the balance of power in Europe. The Emperor's position was weakened, whereas the French recovered their ascendancy in Europe. The Bourbon powers had cemented their alliance in a successful war. In contrast, their traditional opponents, the British, the Dutch, and the Austrians, were more divided than ever. By misjudging the intentions of Fleury and by pursuing a policy of neutrality,

Walpole had not averted a war with France and Spain but had postponed it to less favourable circumstances. He had encouraged the Bourbon powers to believe that they had no need to fear Britain and that they could later challenge the Pragmatic Sanction with impunity. When the War of the Austrian Succession broke out on the death of the Emperor in 1740, the British, Dutch, and Austrians were still divided. The Bourbon powers, on the other hand, were strengthened and encouraged by their victories in the War of the Polish Succession.

It did not take long before Walpole began to suffer the adverse consequences of his policy of neutrality during the fighting of 1733–5. The King and Walpole's ministerial colleagues, notably Newcastle and Hardwicke, were no longer so ready to accept his advice on foreign affairs and began raising objections to his pacific policies. The parliamentary Opposition and public opinion in general, particularly the merchant community, increasingly argued that Britain might have to fight in order to protect her commercial and colonial interests from the aggressive policies of France and Spain. While Walpole was being pressed by his domestic critics to take a more belligerent attitude towards the Bourbon powers in future, the great powers in Europe had become convinced by his recent conduct that he would avoid war at all costs. Britain's traditional allies, the Dutch and the Austrians, no longer trusted her to fight to preserve their territories or the balance of power in Europe. This meant that Britain was left without a reliable friend in Europe. On the other hand, France and Spain were confident they could ignore any threat from Britain while Walpole remained in power. France believed that Britain would not guarantee the Pragmatic Sanction and so the Habsburg territories could be easily dismantled on the death of the Emperor. Spain was encouraged by her alliance with France and by the recent weakness of Walpole to believe that she had no need to make any important concession to Britain in order to settle the long-standing commercial disputes between the two countries. It was a combination of Spanish intransigence and the more belligerent mood in Britain, both of which stemmed from

Walpole's policy of neutrality during the War of the Polish Succession, that caused the Anglo–Spanish war of 1739 and ultimately ended Walpole's long career in power.

Ever since Britain had wrung commercial concessions out of Spain at the end of the War of the Spanish Succession the two countries had been in dispute about the regulation of this trade. Spain complained that the limited privileges she had granted to the South Sea Company were being systematically abused. The company, it was asserted, was not paying the King of Spain his share of the profits on its legitimate trade with Spanish America and was engaged in much illicit trade as well. In addition, large numbers of British merchants were illegally trading with Spanish America. Britain replied to these accusations by claiming that the South Sea Company was unable to make her trade profitable because of the restrictions imposed by Spain and that many innocent British traders operating in West Indian waters were suffering from the attentions of the Spanish coastguard patrols, which were intent on preserving Spain's monopoly of trade with her colonial possessions. Both countries had reasonable grounds for complaint and so it proved extraordinarily difficult to achieve a satisfactory compromise. Throughout the 1730s attempts were made to reach a settlement, but to no avail. Both sides became increasingly embittered and distrustful, and contemplated war. For a time, during the negotiations of 1738–9, it looked as if war might be averted. By the terms of the Convention of the Pardo, Spain agreed to pay £95,000 compensation to British traders, if the South Sea Company acknowledged that it owed the King of Spain £68,000 in unpaid duties on its trade with Spanish America.

Parliament accepted these terms, but not before the Opposition had demonstrated their complete hostility towards such a settlement. For some years the Opposition and the merchant community had been protesting at the violent methods used by the Spanish coastguards to disrupt Britain's lucrative and legitimate trade in the West Indies. Their campaigns aroused considerable public sympathy for the fate of British merchant seamen, such as the celebrated Captain Jenkins, who was supposed to have had his ear cut off when his ship was boarded by a Spanish coastguard patrol. The strength of public opinion on this issue was demonstrated by a large number of petitions to Parliament from all the important ports in Britain. Feelings ran so high that the nervous Duke of Newcastle was encouraged to criticize Walpole's pacific gestures towards Spain, and the resistance of the South Sea Company to the demands made by the King of Spain was stiffened. For the first time, Newcastle was ready to dispute openly with Walpole in the meetings of the inner cabinet. He protested that the Convention did not settle all of Britain's disputes with Spain and he stressed that Spain must not be allowed to think that Britain would not fight to protect her vested interests. The South Sea Company, for its part, refused to pay the British Government the sum of £68,000, which it owed to the King of Spain, so that this money could be used to pay off most of Spain's compensation to the British merchants who had suffered at the hands of the Spanish coastguards.

Spain, probably encouraged by her alliance with France and the recent indecisiveness of Walpole's foreign policy, replied by threatening to rescind the commercial privileges of the South Sea Company. Walpole, with extreme reluctance, finally decided that he could not retreat any further. If he allowed Spain to break a formal treaty signed in 1713, he would lose the confidence of the Commons. The dangerous breach within the ministry, the increasing popularity of the Opposition's campaign, and the aggressive mood of the country, forced his hand. He could no longer avoid war and stay in power. In October 1739, showing every mark of repugnance, Walpole bowed to the pressure coming from all sides and agreed to a war which he had desperately tried to avoid. By so doing, he swung public opinion behind him and temporarily reasserted his political authority over his colleagues and over Parliament. After years of indecision and inept diplomacy Walpole at last stood firm when it was too late to convince Spain of the seriousness of his resolve.

Walpole's ministry soon showed itself incapable of winning

the war against Spain, and its failures lost it the confidence of Parliament. Admiral Vernon struck a serious blow at the Spanish position at Porto Bello in December 1739, but this was the only success achieved while Walpole remained in power. His administration lacked the will and the capacity to fight a decisive war on land or sea. Walpole himself was preoccupied with his fear of a foreign invasion combined with a Jacobite rebellion. He wanted to concentrate on defensive measures in case France declared war, although the struggle against Spain was bound to be concentrated in West Indian waters. His control of government policy, however, had been seriously weakened. He was no longer the great power in the inner cabinet. To some extent he had become the unwilling prisoner of his ministerial colleagues, though no other minister could dominate the administration as he had done in the past. Newcastle favoured sending as many troops as possible out to the West Indies, but his arguments were undermined by the failure of the attack on Carthagena and by the ministry's inability to find enough seamen to man the fleet properly. Both the parliamentary Opposition and the merchant community, though they had pressed hard for this war, successfully defeated the Government's measures in 1740 and 1741 to enlist merchant seamen into the fleet. Divided councils and obstructive tactics naturally produced indecisive measures.

To make matters worse, Britain was faced with the prospect of a war against France as well as Spain, and without a friend in Europe to whom she could turn for assistance. The success of French diplomacy in recent years ensured that Britain would find no support from Russia, Prussia, or the Scandinavian powers. The Dutch had already showed their reluctance to fight another war against France, and the Austrians had bitter memories of Britain's neutrality during the War of the Polish Succession. Walpole's policies had led him into the situation which he had always dreaded: a war with two major maritime powers and without a friend in Europe. Britain was saved by the opportune death of the Emperor, Charles VI, in 1740. Frederick the Great of Prussia at once seized this opportunity to attack the Habsburg territories inherited by Maria Theresa. France too decided to take this chance of dismantling the vast Habsburg territories. This War of the Austrian Succession diverted France's attention away from a naval war against Britain and towards the conflict in Germany. This decision provided Britain with an ally in Maria Theresa. These developments, which owed nothing to Walpole's diplomacy, probably saved Britain from disastrous defeats; but they did not ensure her victory in this enlarged conflict. While Walpole remained in power, Britain was too preoccupied with trying to reassert her naval supremacy to be in any position to intervene in Europe. Walpole was only concerned with avoiding invasion. Indeed, he made himself unpopular with Maria Theresa, by urging her to cede part of Silesia to Prussia so that her armies would be free to fight the French, and with the Opposition in Parliament, by agreeing to accept the neutrality of Hanover in this conflict. This attitude lost him the confidence of his Austrian allies and of the Commons. The general election of 1741 saw his majority dwindle as he proved incapable of waging a successful war. By January 1742 the trading cities of Britain, which had helped to push Walpole into this war, now petitioned for greater vigilance in the prosecution of it. Unable to meet their demands, weary of the burdens imposed upon him, and losing the confidence of the Commons, Walpole decided to resign. He left others to continue the War of the Austrian Succession, with mixed success, for another six years. After twenty-one years in power he had paid the penalty for his inept diplomacy.

8   Walpole and his Critics

For more than twenty years Robert Walpole dominated a successful administration, which commanded the support of the King and the confidence of Parliament. During these years he achieved all his major political aims. He restored financial stability after the ravages of war and the disaster of the South Sea Bubble; he avoided war abroad until 1739 and promoted domestic harmony; and he reconciled a majority of the nation to the Hanoverian dynasty, the Revolution Settlement, the Whig supremacy, and to his own powerful position. Many of his contemporaries and nearly all historians have recognized that his objectives were clear and rational, his policies were pragmatic and expedient, and his methods were usually effective. In view of his considerable political success, therefore, it can come as something of a surprise to learn how unpopular he was and how much abuse was heaped upon him. These criticisms have sometimes been ignored and rarely taken seriously because they were made by such ambitious and frustrated politicians and writers as Pulteney, Bolingbroke, Swift, and Pope. The opposition to Walpole was often factious and hypocritical, and it was usually ineffective, but it deserves serious attention. The opposition was not just a small, political and literary circle based in London. Walpole was very unpopular with large sections of the community that were not powerfully represented in Parliament: the lesser gentry and lower clergy of the rural areas and the smaller merchants and craftsmen of the urban centres. These were the men who read the great Opposition journals such as *The Craftsman*, the *London Journal*, and the *London Evening Post*, and the increasing number of provincial newspapers which were hostile to Walpole. The great political and literary figures in the Opposition ranks were only giving voice to some of the misgivings many less articulate men had about the consequences of Walpole's policies. In prose and in verse, in print and on the stage, in street ballads and in cartoons, Walpole was lambasted not only by literary hacks hired by the Opposition, but by many of the greatest writers of the day, including Henry Fielding, John Gay, Alexander Pope, and Jonathan Swift. Their works tell us much about the political climate during Walpole's administration.

The main functions of Walpole's administration were to conduct foreign policy and to raise the revenue needed by the Government. Most of the debates in Parliament and much of the political discussion outside Parliament revolved around these two important issues. Obviously, since he survived so long in power, Walpole performed these duties to the satisfaction of both King and Parliament. There were, of course, occasions when the Opposition could build up a good case against Walpole's financial and foreign policies. In financial matters, for example, Walpole's opponents could criticize his solution to the South Sea Bubble crisis, his excise scheme, and his attempts to protect the interests of the rich at the cost of higher taxation on the majority of the population. In foreign affairs, Walpole could be accused in the 1720s of maintaining a large standing army and paying heavy subsidies to small European states in order to defend the interests of Hanover, and in the 1730s of being so anxious to avoid war that he encouraged the ambitions of the Bourbon powers and left Britain without a friend in Europe.

These were legitimate objections to some of Walpole's actions, but he was almost always in a position to defend himself. If the Opposition's campaign made too much headway, he was always prepared to retreat. This cut the ground from underneath his critics, and so Walpole survived while the Opposition appeared ineffective. Despite their recurring failures to achieve a majority in Parliament against Walpole's policies, the main spokesmen for the Opposition were able to mount a serious and sustained attack on his *political methods*. With some justice they maintained that Walpole was prepared to use any means, no matter how corrupt or dishonest, to monopolize power in his own hands and to perpetuate his administration. They did not object to his avowed aim, which was to secure the Hanoverian Settlement on Revolution principles, but they did reject his assertion that his political methods were the only means to achieve these ends. On the contrary, they argued that Walpole's tactics were a betrayal of Revolution principles and a threat to the stability of the Hanoverian dynasty. Walpole, they constantly reiterated, might proclaim the noble aims of his administration, but his years in office saw such gross abuses of the Government's power that he quite literally threatened the fundamental principles of the constitution and weakened the moral fibre of society.

There was a great deal of evidence to sustain the Opposition's charge that Walpole was attempting to monopolize power and that he would use corrupt means to achieve this end. They argued that Walpole was seeking to act as the King's sole or prime minister. He kept his rivals out of power, he forced men out of office if they disagreed with him, and he weakened the independence of many of the King's ministers by concentrating power in the hands of an inner cabinet for which there was no constitutional justification. He won the King's favour by bribing the royal mistresses, by increasing the civil list, and by spending lavishly to protect the interests of Hanover. Having ingratiated himself at Court, he used his power to enrich himself and to bribe men to support him with their votes in elections and in Parliament. By exploiting government patronage he was able to corrupt sufficient voters and Members of Parliament to sustain him in power.

This charge, that Walpole was a tyrannical minister who maintained himself in power by corrupt means, was a theme which ran through all the speeches and writings of the Opposition. In the pages of *The Craftsman* Walpole was frequently compared to earlier royal favourites who had abused their power, such as Piers Gaveston, Cardinal Wolsey, and the Duke of Buckingham. John Gay, in *The Beggar's Opera*, portrayed

Walpole as a notorious thief in the guise of 'Robin of Bagshot, alias Gorgon, alias Bluff Bob, alias Bob Booty'. One contemporary street-ballad, *Robin will be out at last*, proclaimed:

> Good people draw near
> And a Tale you shall hear,
> A Story concerning one Robin,
> Who, from not worth a Groat,
> A vast fortune has got,
> By Politicks, Bubbles and Jobbing.

> But a few Years ago,
> As we very well know,
> He scarce had a Guinea his Fob in;
> But by bribing of Friends,
> To serve his dark Ends,
> Now worth a full Million is Robin.

All the corrupt techniques by which Walpole built up the Court and Treasury party were highlighted by the Opposition. In several of his plays, notably *Don Quixote in England* and *Pasquin*, Henry Fielding criticized the bribing of voters during election campaigns. Alexander Pope, particularly in his *Epilogue to the Satires*, attacked placemen who would sell their political independence and their virtue to the Court. A contemporary cartoon depicted hordes of servile creatures queueing to kiss Walpole's bare rump from which dropped a stream of golden guineas.

The leaders of the Opposition did not attack bribery and corruption simply because this abuse of power kept Walpole in office. They used such evidence to level two general charges against Walpole of a much more serious nature. They accused him of encouraging a lamentable decline in moral standards and of threatening the nation's liberties by undermining the constitution. It was a constant Opposition theme that Walpole was responsible for the contemporary vices of worshipping idle luxury and pursuing inordinate wealth, while he presided over the decline of the traditional virtues of industry, simplicity, honesty, and patriotism. He was accused of surrounding himself with profligate creatures who would sell their principles and their country for a place or a pension. Even independent back-benchers, such as Lord Egmont, and Government supporters, such as Lord Hervey, admitted that Walpole was served by vicious, debauched, and corrupt men like Giles Earle, Sir George Oxenden, and William Yonge. The Opposition maintained that the whole of society was being undermined by Walpole's willingness to advance such creatures and his attempts to corrupt more honest men.

Corruption on such a scale was possible, according to the Opposition, because Walpole could exploit not only the Crown's patronage, but his close links with the moneyed interest. Indeed, the Financial Revolution, and the whole system of public credit and paper money, were regarded as the real sources of corruption. The moneyed men formed a new interest which had no real stake in the country and which was ready to betray the nation in order to further its own ends. Their example and their support for Walpole weakened the moral fibre of other men and increased the ministry's ability to buy support. In his *Epistle to Bathurst*, Alexander Pope lamented the way this dangerous financial power could be abused by Walpole:

> Blest paper-credit! last and best supply!
> That lends Corruption lighter wings to fly!
> Gold imp'd by thee, can compass hardest things,
> Can pocket States, can fetch or carry Kings;
> A single leaf shall waft an Army o'er,
> Or ship off Senates to a distant Shore;
> A leaf, like Sybil's, scatter to and fro
> Our fates and fortunes, as the winds shall blow:
> Pregnant with thousands flits the Scrap unseen,
> And silent sells a King, or buys a Queen.

The corrupting influence of money was seen not only in Walpole's ability to build up a Court and Treasury party, but in what many commentators regarded as the declining moral standards of the day. If Court and Parliament could be corrupted, then it was feared that no area of public life could be free from

VII   'Excise in Triumph' (1733) – an attack on the economic and political
     consequences of Walpole's Excise Bill of 1733

VIII 'The Festival of the Golden Rump' (1737) – the problems of serving George II. The King is represented as an irascible satyr, Queen Caroline is the high priestess, and Walpole the court magician.

the taint of selfish materialism. The South Sea Bubble confirmed the worst fears of the pessimists who hated the undue political influence of the moneyed men and the low moral standards of the leading Whig politicians. This financial scandal, however, was by no means an isolated example of corruption in high places. Throughout Walpole's administration there were a number of embarrassing disclosures about shady financial practices that convinced the Opposition that there was an alarming degree of corruption in public life. Walpole was not always directly implicated, but he could not readily avoid the charge that his political methods and his debauched associates encouraged this decline in the standards of public morality. Lord Chancellor Macclesfield, not content with the emoluments of his high and profitable office, used his legal patronage to feather his own nest. He made a practice of selling Masterships in Chancery for exorbitant sums, ranging from 1,500 to 5,000 guineas, and then neglected to supervise the Masters' methods of dealing with the money lodged with them by litigants in Chancery. By the time Macclesfield was impeached in 1725 over £100,000 had been embezzled in this way. Walpole had hoped to avoid a trial, but when this proved impossible he made sure that it should be managed by his friends so that nothing further should be attempted than an inquiry into what immediately related to Macclesfield's conduct. When Macclesfield was convicted the King offered to help him pay the fine of £30,000.

Two years later, in 1727, John Ward was expelled from the Commons for fraudulent practices involving the forfeited estates of the former directors of the South Sea Company. In 1731–2 another financial scandal was exposed when the activities of the Charitable Corporation were investigated. It was discovered that this body, which had been established nominally to assist the poor by lending them small sums of money on pledges, was really being exploited to enrich its projectors, who charged very high interest rates. One of those convicted of negligence was Sir Robert Sutton, a supporter of Walpole. Although the minister was unable to prevent Sutton being expelled from the Commons, he was able to save him from any further punishment, and Sutton quietly resumed his place in the Commons after the general election of 1734. In the same session of 1732 Walpole attempted to avoid an inquiry into the fraudulent sale of the confiscated estates of the Earl of Derwentwater, a Jacobite who had been executed for his part in the 1715 rebellion. Once more the Opposition successfully pursued its investigations and two more supporters of Walpole were expelled from the Commons. Yet another major scandal was unearthed in 1733, when the Opposition pressed for an examination of the finances of the York Building Company. It was discovered that the governor and agents of the company had embezzled some of its funds. This success encouraged the Opposition to press for further inquiries into the management of the forfeited estates of the directors of the South Sea Company and of the customs service, but Walpole was able to thwart these efforts.

Nevertheless, enough damaging disclosures about financial corruption were made during the years Walpole was in power to convince many writers, even those not personally embittered by the frustration of their political ambitions, that the standard of public morality was deplorably low. They attacked the vices of the Court, of Parliament, and of London life and offered, in contrast, an ideal picture of rural life that was simple, honest, and virtuous. In Gay's *The Beggar's Opera* the city of London was depicted as being controlled by a gang of thieves. In his odes *On Solitude* and *Windsor Forest*, Alexander Pope praised the virtues of the honest country gentleman. In his *Epistle to Burlington* he maintained that the simple squire benefited the nation more if he lived in rural innocence away from the corrupting power of gold. Samuel Johnson, like Gay and Pope, was another poet who loved London yet abhorred its corrupting influence. In his poem, *London*, written in 1738, he advised honest men to retreat from a city where Walpole and gold ruled all :

> Here let those reign, whom pensions can incite
> To vote a patriot black, a courtier white;
> Explain their country's dear-bought rights away,
> And plead for pirates in the face of day;

With slavish tenets taint our poison'd youth,
And lend a lye the confidence of truth.
Let such raise palaces and manors buy,
Collect a tax, or farm a lottery,
With warbling eunuchs fill a licens'd stage,
And lull to servitude a thoughtless age.

The great writers of the age were nearly all alarmed at the cultural and social consequences of Walpole's political methods. They usually associated with the parliamentary opposition to his administration, even if they were not politically ambitious themselves. While they concentrated on the decline in moral standards, however, their political allies emphasized Walpole's threat to the constitution. The writers appealed to a wider public, whereas politicians such as Pulteney and Bolingbroke had a more limited aim : the votes of the electorate and of the independent backbenchers in the Commons. To succeed in this, they needed to show that Walpole was a danger to the nation's liberties. They maintained that his political methods, if not rejected, would destroy the balanced constitution which had been so carefully safeguarded by the Revolution Settlement. This constitution was able to guarantee both stability and liberty, because it combined the virtues of monarchy, aristocracy, and democracy. The representatives of these three elements – Crown, Lords, and Commons – together formed a mixed government. Their powers, however, were not separated, but balanced. All three joined together to enact laws, though each also had a particular function : the sovereign was the head of the executive, the House of Lords was the supreme court of justice, and the Commons controlled the voting of supplies. Only if these three elements worked in harmony, while also retaining their independent privileges, could the constitution survive. The delicate balance between them had to be preserved to prevent the government from degenerating into a simple form of either monarchy, aristocracy, or democracy that would sacrifice liberty or stability.

This mixed government and balanced constitution was now threatened by Walpole even though he claimed to be defending the Revolution Settlement. The Opposition claimed that Walpole's exploitation of the Crown's patronage to create a powerful Court and Treasury party was undermining the political independence of the Lords and the Commons, making them both subservient to the Court. If Walpole was allowed to destroy the independence of Parliament, then the constitution would be fundamentally altered and the liberties of the subject put in jeopardy. A packed Parliament was worse than no Parliament at all, Walpole's critics maintained, because men would be seduced by the illusion of liberty instead of struggling to achieve it. If Walpole remained much longer in power, then Parliament would no longer be controlled by the trusted representatives of those sections of the community with a real stake in the country's welfare and the nation's liberties. Instead, Parliament would be dominated by courtiers, placemen, financiers, and stockjobbers, who would forever be subservient to a corrupt, tyrannical minister. In other words, unless the Opposition defeated Walpole, political virtue would decline and the constitution would collapse.

The leaders of the Opposition were quite clear as to what policies they should pursue in order to protect the constitution. The Septennial Act should be repealed and replaced by legislation requiring triennial or even annual parliaments, which would make M.P.s more responsive to the electorate to whom they would have to present themselves so frequently. The Government's electoral interest should be weakened by Acts against corrupt practices in elections and by the stringent enforcement of the legislation about the property qualifications of parliamentary candidates. There should be legislation to destroy the Court and Treasury party by excluding placemen and pensioners from the Commons. Investigations should be made into the financial management of the departments of state and the whole system of public credit should be strictly regulated. Finally, the size of the standing army in peace time should be reduced. The defence of the country and the maintenance of law and order should be the responsibility of the country gentlemen acting as J.P.s and serving in the local militia. These demands were in fact the traditional policies of the Country Opposition which had long feared the political encroachments of the Court.

Devising a parliamentary programme to counter Walpole's political methods and to safeguard the balanced constitution was not difficult. The real problem was how to put these policies into action. Clearly it would become more difficult the longer Walpole was allowed to perfect his methods and the longer the opposition to him remained weak and divided. The most pressing tasks for the leading critics of Walpole were to unite the disparate elements of the opposition and convince many of the independent backbenchers to join with them to save the constitution. The need for a united Opposition was therefore plain, but its creation was inhibited by several factors. There were still many Members of Parliament who regarded themselves as either Whigs or Tories and who were still prepared to fight the old party battles. Even within these old party groups there were divisions. The Opposition Whigs included different factions anxious to force their way into power without regard to their allies and radical Whigs who distrusted the 'outs' as much as the 'ins'. The Tories had never patched up the divisions which had crippled them in the last years of Anne's reign. There was a Jacobite faction led by William Shippen and a number of Hanoverian Tory groups with a variety of leaders, including Hanmer, Bromley, and Wyndham. Finally, there was a third major element, the independent country gentlemen. Many of these were reluctant to oppose the King's ministers unless they were convinced that the Government was pursuing disastrous policies. The others were true Country Members, who were critical of all administrations and were ready to support the Opposition's policies which would reduce the power of the Court and the executive. None of the independents, however, had any interest in defeating Walpole in order to replace him with a minister of the same calibre. This made them reluctant to unite with discontented Whigs such as Pulteney, who seemed to be anxious to step into Walpole's shoes.

The need to unite the actual and potential opponents of Walpole exercised the minds of Opposition theorists throughout

Walpole's administration. In the early 1720s two radical Whigs, Thomas Gordon and John Trenchard, wrote 'Cato's Letters', which were published in the *London Journal*, in an effort to unite all honest men, whether Whig, Tory, or independent, against Walpole. Their arguments were developed more fully by Bolingbroke and Pulteney in their contributions to *The Craftsman* in the late 1720s and early 1730s. The case for forgetting old divisions and for creating a new united Opposition was put most forcibly by Bolingbroke in a series of articles in *The Craftsman* entitled 'A Dissertation upon Parties'. In this treatise he argued that the Tories had combined with the Whigs to accomplish the Revolution Settlement and, in doing so, had purged themselves of the old doctrines of divine right and hereditary succession. Furthermore, the differences between the parties over religion had been reconciled by the Toleration Act of 1689. It was therefore absurd to use the old party labels to describe the present contest for power. The majority of the former Whig and Tory parties ought to unite in defence of the constitution and in opposition to a handful of Jacobites on the one hand and Walpole's mercenary detachment on the other. Walpole was trying to retain the old party divisions in order to serve his own selfish ambition. To triumph over such a well-entrenched minister required an Opposition which would rise above the quarrels of Whig and Tory in an attempt to form a new Country Party in defence of the constitution.

Bolingbroke offered a sophisticated analysis of the contemporary political system, but this was not enough to create an effective Opposition. Many backbenchers ignored his advice to abandon the old Whig–Tory disputes. Those who did found that the Country programme was essentially negative. It criticized the abuse of power by the executive, but it did not establish the Opposition's irresistible claim to replace Walpole. Many sincere Country backbenchers suspected that Bolingbroke, Pulteney, and others adopted this programme merely to dress up their own political ambitions in high constitutional principles. Although for a time this Opposition caused the administration considerable trouble and played a large part in the defeat of the excise scheme in 1733, it began to disintegrate after Walpole's success in the general election of 1734. The Opposition revived in the late 1730s when Walpole began to run into difficulties. In 1737 Prince Frederick quarrelled with his parents and joined the Opposition; Queen Caroline, Walpole's principal friend at Court, died; and Walpole's foreign policy ran into increasing hostility.

To take advantage of these developments, Bolingbroke, Pulteney, and the literary critics of Walpole expanded the Country party's platform into a Patriot programme. Instead of being a mere watchdog on the constitution the Patriots tried to provide a more regular, systematic opposition. By gathering around the Prince of Wales they could at least hope that the reversionary interest would ensure that they held office under the next king. The Opposition therefore opened a campaign which praised the heir to the throne and pleaded for a 'Patriot King' to save the nation's liberties. This was the burden of poems, such as Richard Glover's *Leonidas* and some of John Gay's *Fables*, and such plays as James Thomson's *Edward and Eleonora* and David Mallet's *Mustapha* and *Alfred*. The most important contribution to this campaign was Bolingbroke's treatise, *The Idea of a Patriot King*. All the endeavours of this nature, however, were not enough to convince a majority in Parliament that Walpole should be replaced by the leaders of the Opposition. When Walpole eventually fell in 1742, this was not so much a triumph for the Opposition as the consequence of Walpole's failure to win the war against France and Spain. The new administration included very few of the Opposition. It was dominated by Walpole's disciples and it relied heavily on Walpole's political methods. The Opposition had not convinced a majority of the independent backbenchers that Walpole and his methods were a serious threat to the Revolution Settlement and the balanced constitution.

The failure of Walpole's critics owed much to the difficulties which hindered the development of a united Opposition, but it was also due to the success of Walpole's own achievements. Walpole's supreme skill in political management and the general support in Parliament for his financial and foreign policies have already been discussed in the previous chapters. In addition to demonstrating his own ability and pushing through his own policies, however, Walpole also endeavoured to combat the Opposition's campaigns to win over the independent back-benchers and the uncommitted voters. He did this partly by trying to counter the Opposition's propaganda and partly by seeking to exploit the divisions among his opponents.

It is true that Walpole was unable to enlist the support of writers of the calibre of Gay, Fielding, Pope, and Swift, perhaps because their talents were better suited to criticizing an administration and expressing dissatisfaction with contemporary life, but he did not abandon the propaganda field to the Opposition. In fact he hired many able writers to defend the ministry. The pro-Government propagandists were not all second-rate hacks, as has often been maintained. They included such able pamphleteers as Benjamin Hoadly, Lord Hervey, Horatio Walpole, and Robert Walpole himself. The kind of work that they and their allies produced lacked the literary qualities and enduring appeal of some of the contributions by Walpole's critics, but this was not solely due to the lack of available talent. It owed much to Walpole's determination to explain and defend his policies in a straightforward, matter-of-fact style. Much of their work was rational, cogent, and forceful. What it lacked in grace and emotion, it made up for in practical effectiveness. Moreover, Walpole paid heavily to make sure that these works were widely read. Over two thousand copies of each issue of such pro-Government newspapers as the *Free Briton* and the *Daily Courant* were distributed free of charge by the Post Office. Individual pamphlets were given away on an even more lavish scale. More than ten thousand copies of pamphlets which attacked his opponents or defended Walpole's own policies, such as *The Conduct of the Opposition*, *Opposition no proof of Patriotism*, and *The Convention Vindicated*, were given away to peers, M.P.s, clergymen, revenue officers, and men of distinction throughout the country.

Public opinion, or at least the open expression of opinion,

was hostile to Walpole on many occasions, but unless this could be translated into votes in the Commons Walpole's position would remain impregnable. Walpole realized this and concentrated much of his efforts on weakening the impact of the opposition's propaganda on the independent backbenchers. He not only defended the ministry's policies, but sought to justify his political methods on which the Opposition concentrated much of their fire. His close alliance with the moneyed interest, he claimed, was in the best interests of the nation, since it allowed the Government to borrow huge sums of money at reasonable rates of interest. The exploitation of the Government's interest in elections and in Parliament did not indicate that the political system was corrupt. Indeed, it could be regarded as an illustration of domestic harmony, for it showed that many men acknowledged their dependence on the Crown and that the nation was not riven by ideological conflicts. The fact that men accepted patronage from the Crown did not mean that they had sold their political principles. Places and pensions, Walpole maintained, went as rewards to men of fortune, honour, and ability, and not as inducements to make them vote against their private sentiments or the interests of the nation. The Opposition's fears for the constitution were merely a cloak for their selfish political ambitions. Walpole claimed that he was just as convinced of the merits of mixed government and just as devoted to the principles of a balanced constitution as his opponents. Indeed, as the most loyal of Whigs, he could be better trusted to defend the Revolution Settlement than any of his leading critics, many of whom were former Tories. His political methods, which the Opposition described as corrupt, were in fact designed to safeguard the constitution. The size of the Court and Treasury party was grossly exaggerated. It did not provide him with a permanent majority. On the other hand, it did help to preserve the balanced constitution. The Revolution Settlement could not work if Crown, Lords, and Commons were kept entirely separate. Harmonious relations between the three were only possible if the sovereign had a body of loyal supporters in both Houses of Parliament. The real threat was not to the independence of Parliament, as the Opposition claimed, but to the power of the Crown.

Walpole's defence was strong enough to prevent the Opposition securing a majority until 1742. He evidently convinced a sufficient number of his contemporaries to be able to stay in power. Most historians have also accepted the validity of many of his claims. Walpole quite clearly did not secure a majority in Parliament by corrupt means. He won many votes by the reasonableness of his policies and the effectiveness of his arguments. Royal patronage and, to a small extent, open corruption were used to build up the Court and Treasury party, but this body was not as large as the Opposition maintained. Moreover, it was probably the only tool Walpole could use to maintain harmonious relations between Crown and Parliament after the disintegration of the Whig and Tory parties. Without it, the King and his ministers might never have been able to manage Parliament for any length of time and the political influence of the Crown might have been seriously reduced in Walpole's day as it has been since. Thus, Walpole probably did more than the Opposition to preserve the balanced constitution. The recognition of this has led many historians to ignore the arguments of the Opposition spokesman or to regard their claims as being deliberately exaggerated because they could not find other legitimate grounds for attacking Walpole. The Opposition, however, did have a case. Walpole did try to dominate the Government and to keep his rivals out of office. He enriched himself, openly gloried in his power, and rode roughshod over many of his opponents. The size of the Court and Treasury party had increased in recent years and there were many signs of political and financial corruption in public life. These developments had not progressed far enough to undermine the independence of Parliament and the liberties of the nation, but if they had continued unchecked then they might have done so. The Opposition's fears were therefore exaggerated, but they were not entirely without foundation. Walpole managed to answer them effectively, but he never quite silenced them.

Walpole was not content with launching his own propaganda campaign. He also tried to silence his critics by exploiting his advantages as a minister. The patronage at his disposal could be used to buy off some of his critics. His offers to men like John Gay were not attractive enough, but he had more success with Thomas Gordon, whose contributions to 'Cato's Letters' had savaged the Government in the early 1720s. When financial inducements failed, Walpole turned to harassment and intimidation. The Stamp Act of 1725 put up the price of newspapers and temporarily restricted their circulation. The Post Office was instructed to examine all the printed material using its service. Under government orders it deliberately hindered the distribution of the *London Evening Post*, *The Craftsman*, and the *Daily Post* when they were particularly severe in their criticisms of Walpole's administration. The most influential Opposition journal, *The Craftsman*, was such a thorn in Walpole's side that eight writs were issued against the publisher in four years. In 1729 the publisher, Richard Francklin, was eventually brought to trial, but he was acquitted by a jury packed by John Barber, the Lord Mayor of London, who was friendly with the leading opponents of the ministry. Two years later Walpole insisted on another prosecution after he had ensured that the jury would be of a different political persuasion. The Juries Act of 1730 allowed judges to empanel special juries for cases tried at Westminster and increased the property qualifications required by jurors. The political trial that followed in 1731 ended in Francklin being fined and imprisoned, though it did not silence *The Craftsman*. Walpole did not cease his vigilance however. Even provincial publishers, such as John White, who ran the *Newcastle Courant*, found themselves prosecuted for printing material which the Government considered libellous.

Walpole's abuse of his power did not silence the Opposition, but he undoubtedly weakened its impact, especially in London. He was particularly successful in his belated attempts to censor the London stage and in his earlier attempts to control the government of the capital. After the great success in 1728 of John Gay's *The Beggar's Opera*, with its veiled satirical attacks on Walpole, the Government prohibited any public performance of its sequel, *Polly*. This warning did not prevent many other outrageous attacks on Walpole, particularly a series of plays in the 1730s by Henry Fielding. When it was discovered in 1737 that there was a plan to stage *The Festival of the Golden Rump*, a scurrilous, even obscene, attack on Walpole, the ministry rushed the Licensing Act through Parliament. In future, before any new play could be performed, it had to secure the approval of the Lord Chamberlain. He could be relied upon to censor all productions which attacked the Government. Walpole had saved himself from any further stage productions critical of him or his administration.

The writers for the London press and the London stage were not the only critics of Walpole who could exert pressure on the ministry from outside Parliament. Many London merchants, particularly those who were not attached to the great financial and trading corporations, were hostile to Walpole's financial, commercial, and foreign policies. They were among the most active petitioners of Parliament against the actions proposed by Walpole's ministry. Walpole tried to weaken their influence by re-modelling the government of London. He deliberately attempted to increase the power of the rich, City financiers and merchants, who were more conservative and on good terms with the Government, while reducing the influence of the less wealthy tradesmen, craftsmen, and merchants. In 1725 the City Elections Act gave the twenty-six aldermen, who were usually among the richest citizens of London, the right to veto the legislation of the Common Council, whose 234 members represented the commercial interests of the thousands of freemen of the capital. For a time this Act seriously curtailed the political freedom of the Common Council. The petitions and protests from the commercial interest were curbed, while the power of Walpole's allies over the City's government and over its representatives in Parliament was increased. Within a few years, however, Walpole's opponents were beginning to infiltrate the Court of Aldermen. London played a major role in forcing Walpole to abandon the excise scheme of 1733 and in pushing him into a war against Spain in 1739.

Walpole did not just counter the arguments of his critics
or harass their attempts to mount a sustained propaganda campaign. He also sought to destroy the credibility of the Opposition as an alternative administration. One certain way of
weakening the impact of the Opposition on the independent
backbenchers in the Commons was to play upon the natural
jealousies and differences among his critics. Walpole excited the
suspicions of the genuine Country backbenchers about the selfish
political ambitions of the leading spokesmen of the Opposition.
They never lost their fears that politicians such as Pulteney and
Wyndham were using them simply as a means of gaining power.
These discontented 'outs' were prepared to adopt demands for
Place Bills and annual parliaments in order to embarrass the
Government, not to safeguard the constitution. Subsequent
events confirmed these fears and Walpole's efforts to exploit
them. After the fall of Walpole in 1742 several of the Opposition
leaders gained office, but made no attempt to implement the
Country or Patriot programme.

Walpole had even more success in dividing the Opposition
along Whig and Tory lines. He claimed that the differences
between the two parties were as great as ever. The Tories could
not be trusted because of their Jacobite sympathies. The ever-
present Jacobite threat therefore meant that the Hanoverian
succession and the Revolution Settlement could only be defended
by the political supremacy of the Whigs. Many of the Opposition leaders, including Bolingbroke, Wyndham, and Shippen,
were Jacobites or ex-Jacobites. The Opposition Whigs, because
of their association with such men, could no longer be trusted
to defend Revolution principles. If the Opposition Whigs wished
to serve the Hanoverian monarchy they must end their alliance
with the Tories. The activities of Bolingbroke, a former Secretary of State to the Pretender, gave Walpole several opportunities to embarrass the Opposition and to divide them into Whig
and Tory camps. He openly accused Bolingbroke of being so
embittered at his failure to return to power that, in an effort
to gain revenge, he deliberately incited the Dunkirk inquiry of
1730 and the opposition to the excise scheme in 1733. In the

debate in 1734 to repeal the Septennial Act, Walpole ignored the
real issue in dispute and launched instead into a blistering attack
on Bolingbroke. He accused him of continuing his work for the
Pretender through his well-known association with the French
ambassador. Bolingbroke's reputation was destroyed so effectively that he became a liability to the Opposition and retreated
once more to France. At the same time, Pulteney, Carteret, and
other Opposition Whigs were encouraged to abandon their close
ties with the Tories in order to improve their chances of gaining office under a Hanoverian monarch.

Walpole deliberately and unscrupulously used the Jacobite
scare to smear the reputations of some of his leading critics
and to divide the Opposition into mutually hostile factions. This
policy, however, would not have been so successful if the
genuine alarm about Jacobitism had not been widespread. Indeed, there are many indications that Walpole himself shared
this fear and did not simply exploit it in a cynical fashion. In
1722 such fears were reinforced when a Jacobite conspiracy
was uncovered. Several prominent Tories, including Bishop
Atterbury, Lord Orrery, and Lord North and Grey, were deeply
implicated in this plot. Walpole gave this case his undivided
attention, partly to exploit it for his own political advantage
but also because he always feared that the Hanoverian succession, the Revolution Settlement, and his own power might all
be destroyed by a successful Jacobite rebellion. Throughout his
administration Walpole spared neither time nor money in his
efforts to forestall any Jacobite plot. He organized a counter-
espionage system throughout Europe. Agents were placed in
most of the capitals and postmasters on the main postal routes
were bribed to examine all potential Jacobite correspondence.
It was probably this vigilance which provided him with information about Bolingbroke's near-treasonable correspondence with
the French Government in the early 1730s. Any scrap of intelligence about Jacobite activities was magnified by Walpole's
deep-seated anxiety and by his desire to remind the public of
the threat they faced. He may have exaggerated the Jacobite
menace, but his vigilance played a part in reducing the danger.

The threat was real enough, however, to enable Walpole to keep the Opposition almost permanently divided. Walpole's fears, and those of many of his contemporaries, were confirmed and justified by the Jacobite rebellion of 1745.

9 Walpole in Power (1721-42)

Walpole dominated the Government and the political scene for more than twenty years. This unparalleled achievement was due to several factors which have already been analysed in detail. Royal favour made him the leading minister in the Government. Crown patronage gave him a solid base in both Houses of Parliament, and he won over many independent backbenchers by the reasonableness of his financial and foreign policies and by the persuasiveness of his arguments. Moreover, his skill in managing the Commons and in dividing his opponents extricated him from a number of situations where he faced defeat and the loss of power. Nonetheless, his success was not easily gained and he could never be assured of victory. His position could be threatened on several fronts. He could lose favour at Court, he could face a revolt by his cabinet colleagues, his policies and decisions could be rejected by the independent backbenchers, or the Opposition spokesmen could turn a majority of the Commons or the electorate against him. Walpole was rarely entirely safe from all these challenges, and his power fluctuated according to the strength and nature of the threat to his authority. His remarkable political talents enabled him to beat off these attacks when they came from only one or two directions. He finally fell from power when he was opposed on all fronts. He lost influence at Court and in the cabinet. The independent backbenchers became disenchanted with his conduct of the War of the Austrian Succession and the Opposition at last persuaded more of the electorate and a majority of the Commons to vote against him.

Walpole had not come to power in 1721 on a great wave

of popularity, nor in answer to a widespread demand for his services as the only man who could save the country from ruin after the disaster of the South Sea Bubble. In fact, he had forced his way to the head of the administration against the bitter opposition of ministerial rivals and against a background of almost uncontrollable parliamentary and public rage against the Government. Nevertheless, the crisis created by the bursting of the South Sea Bubble gave him the opportunity to stamp his authority on the ministry and he seized this chance with both hands. His success in stabilizing the nation's finances, the death of several of his main ministerial rivals, and the divisions among his parliamentary opponents enabled Walpole to ride out the political storm of 1720 to 1722. This remarkable achievement won him the full support of George I for the first time and helped him to secure a more manageable House of Commons after the general election of 1722.

Walpole's first two crucial years in power showed that the parliamentary Opposition was disorganized and ineffective. Many of the Opposition Whigs believed that Walpole could be easily defeated by intriguing against him at Court. Their tactical error and their distrust of the political aims of the Tory Opposition, especially after Walpole's discovery of a Jacobite plot in 1722, led them to neglect the campaign against the ministry in Parliament. With the leading critics of Walpole hopelessly divided among themselves, many independent backbenchers either swung behind the ministry or failed to turn up regularly to the debates in the Commons. The parliamentary Opposition shrank to insignificant proportions by the mid-1720s and Walpole could count upon a stable majority in both chambers. A more serious threat to Walpole came, in fact, from within the ministry.

Sunderland had never accepted Walpole's return to power, but his sudden death ended his political challenge. His demise left Lord Carteret as the main rival to the authority of the Walpole-Townshend partnership. Carteret, the Secretary of State for the Southern Department, was a man of wit, intelligence, and charm. He spoke fluent French and German, and had considerable knowledge of German affairs. These gifts made him influential at Court, but, in Walpole's eyes, the real danger was Carteret's overbearing manner and his efforts to conduct foreign policy without reference to his chief ministerial colleagues, Walpole and Townshend. In particular, his foreign policy aimed at safeguarding the interests of Hanover by securing the friendship of the Emperor and opposing the ambitions of Russia in the Baltic. Walpole regarded this policy as a threat to his plans to retain the friendship of France and as liable to embroil Britain in the complicated affairs of northern Europe. Any military or financial commitment in the area would leave Walpole with the difficult task of raising the necessary revenue from a House of Commons which was suspicious of any policy that smacked of sacrificing British interests to protect Hanover. Fortunately, Townshend was able to combat Carteret's influence with George I and to persuade the King to pursue a more cautious and less expensive foreign policy.

Townshend's triumph seriously undermined Carteret's influence and forced him to desperate measures to restore his credit at Court. All his moves, however, were skilfully countered by Walpole. When he advised the British ambassador to France, who was one of his political allies, to press the Regent to grant a dukedom to the future son-in-law of George I's mistress, the Countess von Platen, Walpole sent his brother Horatio to Paris to scotch this plan. When these hopes were dashed, Carteret retaliated by seeking to create serious political problems for Walpole. He deliberately encouraged his Irish allies, the Brodricks, to continue their opposition to William Wood's patent to mint cheap copper coins for use in Ireland. The Irish boycotted the new coinage and the parliament in Dublin refused to pass any money bills until their grievances had been redressed. This crisis forced Walpole to retreat and withdraw Wood's patent, but he had the delightful and ironic satisfaction of dumping the Irish problem into Carteret's lap. George I, embarrassed by Carteret's recent actions, was persuaded, in April 1724, to remove him from his post as Secretary of State and to appoint him Lord Lieutenant of Ireland. Since he was determined not to be forced even further into the political wilderness, Carteret had to help Walpole to solve the problem in Ireland. This did not stop him welcoming and perhaps inciting the resistance in Scotland to Walpole's malt tax of 1725. Walpole certainly held Carteret's ally, the Duke of Roxburgh, who was the Secretary of State for Scotland, responsible for the failure to prevent the rioting which broke out in Glasgow. The King was persuaded to dismiss Roxburgh and to leave his office vacant. The management of Scotland was then put into the hands of Walpole's political allies, Argyll and Islay.

Having outmanoeuvred Carteret and his friends, Walpole set about consolidating his position as the King's First Minister. The political world was clearly shown that the way to promotion and advancement lay through the good offices of Walpole. He himself was made a Knight of the Garter, a rare honour for a commoner. His eldest son, Robert, was made a baron because Walpole himself could not afford to move to the Lords when his talents were invaluable in the Commons. His friends and allies were also rewarded. Horatio Walpole, the Duke of Devonshire, and Bishop Gibson were all given positions of influence and power. Walpole's influence over such appointments naturally encouraged many ambitious politicians to offer their services to the ministry. Faced with more candidates than vacancies, Walpole naturally chose to reward those who would accept his political leadership rather than the more able men who might wish to challenge his authority.

When Carteret was removed from his position as Secretary of State in 1724, Walpole secured this post for the Duke of Newcastle. While lacking neither commonsense nor judgement, Newcastle was usually too timid to take important political decisions on his own initiative and he was also amenable to flattery and persuasion. Indeed, for more than a decade he was one of Walpole's most reliable ministerial colleagues. Only very cautiously and reluctantly did he start taking an independent line. His willingness to bow to Walpole's authority was only one of the reasons for his promotion. Walpole was well aware of Newcastle's ability as an electoral manager and of his personal control over twelve to sixteen seats. Newcastle himself was a capable administrator and a regular debater in the Lords, but he also brought into the Walpole camp the talents of his younger brother, Henry Pelham, and his closest friend, Philip Yorke. Henry Pelham was at first rewarded with the relatively minor post of Secretary at War, but he soon became one of Walpole's most important lieutenants in the Commons. He revealed a passion for administrative detail, a shrewd understanding of the independent backbenchers, and a strong sense of political loyalty. Philip Yorke, later Earl of Hardwicke, entered the ministry as Attorney-General in 1724, but later served as Lord Chief Justice, and then Lord Chancellor. Walpole gained the services of a highly respected lawyer, an able debater, and a cautious, time-serving politician. He could hardly have asked for more.

Having strengthened his ministry with the Pelham interest, Walpole could afford to frustrate the political ambitions of potential rivals. He decided not to bring his old friend and colleague, William Pulteney, into the ministry. Although he was subsequently accused of being jealous of Pulteney's ability, particularly his eloquence and his understanding of the Commons, Walpole was really afraid of Pulteney's political ambitions. Pulteney was not primarily interested in wealth or prestige. He wanted the power to influence and shape the policies of the Government. This persuaded Walpole to keep him out of office. The same consideration led him to keep Bolingbroke out of Parliament altogether. The former Secretary of State to the Pretender secured a pardon in 1723 after bribing the Duchess of Kendal, one of the King's mistresses; but Walpole made sure that he never recovered a seat in Parliament. Bolingbroke could only retaliate with his pen, which he used to persuade his Tory friends to join Pulteney and the Opposition Whigs in a parliamentary campaign against Walpole.

Before this new parliamentary opposition could make much headway in Parliament, Walpole had to face a much greater challenge at Court. In the summer of 1727 George I died on his annual visit to Hanover, and Walpole's days in office appeared to be over. The new King, George II, had not forgiven Walpole for deserting him in 1720 and for advising him to submit to his father. It was generally expected that he would dismiss Walpole and replace him with his own favourite, Spencer Compton, the Speaker of the House of Commons. Walpole himself feared that he would be laid aside, but he was determined not to give up his place without a fight. As soon as he heard of the death of George I, he rushed to Court to ingratiate himself with the new King and Queen. Fortunately, George II realized that it would be unwise to remove Walpole from power at once, before Compton was prepared to assume his new responsibilities. After several consultations with the two men, the King was left in no doubt as to their respective political and financial talents. Compton proved himself unfit to draw up the King's Speech to the Privy Council and to Parliament without the assistance of Walpole, whereas the latter, his confidence rapidly returning, won the King's favour by offering to persuade Parliament to vote an increased civil list. Walpole's influence at Court was greatly strengthened by the support he gained from Queen Caroline. Walpole had long appreciated the hold which she had over her husband, and he had been busily cultivating her favour while Compton made the mistake of paying court to Mrs Howard, the King's mistress. The Queen was not only motivated by personal resentment, but recognized the superior gifts of Walpole. A woman of strong character and great strength of purpose, she was an excellent judge of men and affairs. She soon joined Walpole in undermining Compton's credit with the King, and for the next ten years she was Walpole's greatest supporter at Court. Compton was promoted to the peerage as Baron, later Earl, of Wilmington, but this honour sensibly reduced his political influence, since the King's chief minister needed to be able to stamp his authority on the Commons. Wilmington remained on friendly terms with George II, though he was no longer a serious rival to Walpole.

Rapidly confirmed as George II's chief minister, Walpole was able to exploit the King's patronage in the general election of 1727. His electoral managers undoubtedly secured the ministry a safe majority, but, with about 150 new Members in the Commons, Walpole could not be certain how strong the Opposition might be in the next few years. Indeed, his corrupt electoral methods encouraged the Opposition to campaign against the undue and dangerous influence of the Court that threatened the independence of Parliament. Moreover, although he was still First Lord of the Treasury and the most influential politician at Court and in the cabinet, his power had been reduced by the death of George I. While there was now the nucleus of a potential Opposition at Court, the more serious threat came from the reviving Opposition in the Commons. This was ably led by William Pulteney, Samuel Sandys, and William Wyndham, and brilliantly inspired by Bolingbroke and the other contributors to *The Craftsman*. The first two or three parliamentary sessions of the new reign saw the achievement of much closer and more more effective co-operation between the malcontent Whigs and the Hanoverian Tories. This new danger to Walpole was largely due to the deterioration in the diplomatic situation, which threatened the peace of Europe and the safety of Britain's trade. The ministry was accused of risking war with both Spain and the Emperor, while allowing these two powers to interfere with Britain's trade with the West and East Indies respectively. The Opposition was not united on what foreign policy the country should pursue, but, for the first time since 1721, Walpole was forced onto the defensive.

Walpole clearly appreciated the political problems created for him by the uncertain situation in Europe and the Opposition's campaign. Townshend's risky and expensive foreign policy compelled him to ask Parliament to vote heavy Bills of Supply and to accept a large standing army in time of peace. These demands irritated the independent backbenchers and made them more receptive to the Opposition's claims that the ministry was sacrificing the country's interests while maintaining itself in power by corrupt means. Walpole, ever sensitive to the mood of the Commons, realized that he would have to jettison Townshend's foreign policy and settle the outstanding disputes in Europe if he were to retain the confidence of the House.

It was this determination that led him to sign the Treaty of Seville with Spain in 1729 and to open negotiations with the Emperor that eventually led to the second Treaty of Vienna in 1731. Walpole regarded these settlements as major diplomatic triumphs, but he eventually paid a heavy price for them. In the long run his sudden plunge into the conduct of foreign affairs lost him the friendship of France, though, in the short term, the breach with Townshend and the criticisms of the Opposition appeared more serious. Fortunately for Walpole, the Secretary of State quietly retired from active politics and did not indulge in any serious intrigue at Court that might have damaged the First Minister's influence. The Opposition, however, was encouraged by what it regarded as Walpole's mismanagement of foreign affairs, and it began to eat into the ministry's comfortable majority in the Commons. Nonetheless, Walpole was never in serious danger in the debates on his foreign policy, because he had succeeded in avoiding war and in reducing the burden of direct taxation on the gentry to its lowest level since the Revolution.

The parliamentary Opposition, however, was able to force Walpole onto the defensive and to increase its strength in the Commons. In 1730 the Opposition attacked the Government's decision to hire thousands of Hessian mercenaries and, in one division, cut the ministry's majority to less than seventy. This was followed up by an inquiry into the Government's failure to prevent the French repairing the fortifications of Dunkirk. On this emotive issue many independent backbenchers wavered in their allegiance to the ministry. Only by an intensive lobbying campaign, by a shabby procedural manoeuvre to prevent the Opposition dividing the Commons on a motion highly critical of the ministry, and by making great play with Bolingbroke's clandestine and suspicious role in bringing forward this whole debate, was Walpole able to extricate himself from this crisis. He was not, however, able to prevent the Opposition pushing such popular measures as Pension and Place Bills through the House.

Walpole's first response to this new danger in the Commons was to strengthen his control over the ministry. When Townshend resigned in 1730 he was replaced by the more complaisant William Stanhope, who was elevated to the peerage as Lord Harrington. Carteret, a potential threat to Walpole's recently established control of foreign policy, was finally disgraced and lost his position as Lord Lieutenant of Ireland. Horatio Walpole was brought home from Paris to strengthen the ministry's team of spokesmen for foreign affairs. His place in France was taken by Lord Waldegrave, while Sir Thomas Robinson replaced Waldegrave at Vienna. Both of these diplomats were ready to serve Walpole without seeking to control the ministry's foreign policy. Two of Walpole's most loyal allies in the Commons, Henry Pelham and Sir William Strickland, were promoted to Paymaster-General and Secretary at War respectively. Having created a stronger and more reliable ministerial team to reply to his critics in Parliament, Walpole then set about restoring his safe majority in the Commons by settling the outstanding disputes between the great powers of western Europe. The second Treaty of Vienna, signed in 1731, pleased backbench opinion by reversing Britain's recent policy of hostility towards the Emperor and by securing the abolition of the Ostend East India Company. Some of Walpole's colleagues rightly feared that he had alienated France by this treaty, but it proved so acceptable to the Commons that not one of them was prepared to challenge his decision.

Walpole's diplomatic triumph gave him considerable confidence and encouraged him to seek a similar success on the domestic front. He planned an important overhaul of the revenue system that would allow him to reduce the land tax to a mere one shilling in the pound while also making the collection of indirect taxes more efficient. To make up for the reduced revenue from the land tax, the salt duty, which had been abolished in 1730, was to be restored, and the excise scheme, which had applied to tea, chocolate, and cocoa since 1724, was to be extended to wine and tobacco. Despite the fiscal merits of this scheme, Walpole soon discovered that he had presented his parliamentary opponents with an issue which could arouse intense emotions. The Opposition soon persuaded the public at large that these inland duties on items of consumption would result in an unequal financial burden on the poor, an unwarranted interference with honest and busy traders, and an army of government officials to collect them. Excise officers, appointed by ministerial patronage, were depicted as instruments of government corruption and oppression.

The Opposition's campaign began when Walpole moved to restore the salt duty in 1732. In one division on this motion the ministry's majority slumped to an alarming twenty-nine votes. This naturally encouraged the Opposition to step up its attacks on the ministry, but Walpole refused to take seriously the threat to his majority in the Commons. Over-confident, even arrogant, he remained determined to extend the excise scheme to wine and tobacco. By the time the Tobacco Bill was introduced in the Commons, in March 1733, the Opposition had persuaded the merchants of London and other ports to prepare petitions against it and had convinced many people that the excise scheme was a threat to the independence of the Commons and to the delicate balance of the constitution. The whole political nation was aroused and gripped by a ferment greater than at any time since the bursting of the South Sea Bubble.

Despite the clamour, Walpole remained confident, even complaisant, about his ability to steer his Tobacco Bill through the Commons. He certainly introduced this bill with great force and clarity, and he was satisfied with his initial majority of sixty-one. The Opposition responded by redoubling its efforts and the disorder throughout the country increased. Petitions and deputations were sent up to Westminster, ministerial pamphlets defending the bill were solemnly burned by several borough corporations, and a disorderly mob began to appear on the streets of London. These clear manifestations of the unpopularity of Walpole's scheme gave his critics at Court, who had previously lacked a suitable opportunity, a chance to undermine his influence with the King. Scarborough, Chesterfield, Stair, Bolton, and other peers with some credit at Court began to express their hostility to the excise scheme, while the Earl of

Wilmington and several bishops showed signs of abandoning their support for Walpole's administration. For the first time, Walpole had to fear for his authority at Court and his majority in the Lords. When his majority in the Commons was reduced to an alarming sixteen votes in the debate on the Tobacco Bill on 5 April 1733, Walpole decided to retreat rather than risk a defeat from which he might never recover.

In fighting for his political life, Walpole showed once more that he had no equal when it came to managing the House of Commons. After warning his closest political friends that he was ready to sound a retreat, he moved, on 11 April, that the next reading of the Tobacco Bill should be postponed until 12 June. The parliamentary session would be over before then, and so the bill was being quietly abandoned, without giving the Opposition the satisfaction of defeating it on the floor of the Commons. Nevertheless, Walpole's tactical retreat was received with intense jubilation in Parliament and in many parts of the country. When Walpole left the Commons after making his announcement, he was jostled by the mob which had been surrounding the chamber. He might have been severely injured if he had not been protected and hustled away by a few friends. The crisis in the Commons, however, might have ended, despite the Opposition's attempts to prolong it, if Henry Pelham had not blundered. On 20 April, during Walpole's absence from the chamber, he accepted the Opposition's demands for an inquiry into the alleged abuses practised by the customs service and for a ballot as the means of choosing the twenty-one commissioners to carry out this investigation. With a superb display of political management Walpole retrieved the situation and secured the election of his list of twenty-one candidates, all of whom were placemen. He called a mass meeting of his potential supporters and warned them of the danger of letting the Opposition defeat the ministry. Many of the Government's critics were Tories who had no love for the present Establishment. It was therefore necessary for all the friends of the administration to support the Revolution Settlement, the Whig Supremacy, and the Hanoverian succession by voting for the ministry's list of candidates. Walpole's brilliant speech had the desired effect. His entire list was carried by a majority which never fell below eighty-five votes.

Walpole had clearly survived the crisis in the Commons, but he also needed to reassert his authority at Court and in the Lords. As soon as he had postponed the next reading of the Tobacco Bill, Walpole turned on those Court peers who had expressed their opposition to this measure. On 13 April the King was persuaded to dismiss Chesterfield and Clinton, and to warn several other peers about their future conduct. Wilmington and Dorset quickly came to heel, but several other Court peers continued to oppose Walpole's policies. Their disloyalty encouraged the Opposition in the Lords to bring up an old grievance: the management of the confiscated estates of the former directors of the South Sea Company. On 24 May 1733 the ministry tried to thwart an Opposition motion to interrogate one of the directors of the company, but it failed on a tied vote of seventy-five peers on either side. This was the first Government defeat in the Lords for many years and Walpole was understandably concerned. The Opposition in the Lords not only included the old stalwarts and recent recruits such as Chesterfield, but staunch Court peers such as Argyll and Scarborough. After considerable lobbying, and after putting heavy pressure on all those peers who feared to lose their places and pensions, Walpole narrowly frustrated the Opposition's campaign; but only by seventy-five votes to seventy. Those defectors whose support was not essential to him were treated ruthlessly by an angry Walpole. Montrose, Marchmont, Stair, Bolton, and Cobham all lost their places. On the other hand, those who had showed signs of going into opposition but whose support was indispensable, such as Argyll, Islay, and Wilmington, were flattered by further honours from the King. The ministry was also strengthened by the creation of four new peers, including Hardwicke and Hervey, in 1734. Thus, Walpole was saved by the loyalty of the King and of the inner ring of ministers, though, for the first time, he faced an effective Opposition in the Lords that included several able Whig peers.

The Opposition as a whole was dejected by the ease with which Walpole had extricated himself from the greatest political crisis he had faced for more than ten years. While he endeavoured to exploit the divisions among his opponents into Whig and Tory factions, before the 1734 general election, Bolingbroke and others laboured to destroy these distinctions which were weakening the Opposition. During the 1734 session the early debates on foreign affairs and on the size of the standing army showed that the Opposition had no clear alternative to the policies pursued by Walpole, and its leading spokesmen were frequently at odds with each other. With the outbreak of the War of the Polish Succession, Bolingbroke and Wyndham advocated a policy of neutrality, whereas Pulteney pressed the Government to assist the candidate supported by Austria. Most backbenchers preferred the ministry's strategy of keeping up the strength of the armed forces while avoiding any active intervention on the Continent. Their confidence in Walpole's foreign policy may have been misplaced, but it undoubtedly strengthened his hand in the struggle going on at Court. Both George II and Queen Caroline were anxious to assist the Emperor, and several of their ministers agreed with them. Walpole was able to resist this pressure by pointing out the political dangers of engaging in a major European war when Britain's interests were not directly involved and when there was a general election in the offing.

The Opposition's failures sparked off mutual recriminations among its leaders. Pulteney lashed out at his Tory allies for still being too much attached to the doctrine of passive obedience and hostile to the principles of the Revolution Settlement. Walpole exploited these divisions when the Opposition moved, in March 1734, to repeal the Septennial Act in the hope that more frequent general elections would reduce the degree of electoral corruption. The highlight of the debate in the Commons was the clash between Walpole and Sir William Wyndham. The Tory leader not only protested at the amount of government interference with the freedom of elections, but savaged Walpole's personal reputation. Walpole's reply electrified the House. He completely ignored the real issue at stake and deliberately set about driving a deep wedge between his Whig and Tory critics by launching a blistering attack on Boling-broke. His hated enemy had foolishly played into Walpole's hands by engaging in secret communications with the French court and accepting money in return for the information he supplied. Bolingbroke had not committed treason, though Wal-pole was not aware of the full extent of his relations with the French; but the minister's hints in this debate were enough. In view of Bolingbroke's past conduct and the unsettled state of affairs of Europe, Walpole's attack was enough to blast the remains of Bolingbroke's reputation with the independent back-benchers and to embarrass the whole Opposition. The discon-tented Whigs began to regard Bolingbroke and the Tories as more of a liability than an asset.

The divisions between the Opposition groups did nothing to improve their chances in the 1734 general election, whereas Walpole worked hard to dispense the Government's patron-age to the best electoral advantage. There was not enough pat-ronage to guarantee Walpole a majority from the general election, but the shrewd distribution of it could secure the maxi-mum amount of goodwill from those rewarded or given promises. No one knew better than Walpole and his electoral agents how to achieve this, and never before had they worked so hard. The Opposition was hardly less active in its campaign against government corruption and the complete domination of the political life of the nation by one man. As a result of the determined efforts of both sides the electoral campaign was expensive, heated, and, in some constituencies, violent. The Opposition scored a number of triumphs, notably in London, the larger boroughs, and most of the counties. John Scrope, Wal-pole's right-hand man at the Treasury, was defeated at Bristol and had to find another seat. Walpole even lost control of the county seats of Norfolk, but the ministry's supporters retained their influence in most of the small boroughs. Walpole's majority was probably reduced to about seventy-five, but this was quite enough to keep him safely in power. In the Lords his position was actually strengthened, since he was able to secure the election of all sixteen Scottish representative peers put forward by the ministry. The relative failure of the Opposition, after entertaining high hopes of defeating Walpole, demoralized its leading spokesmen. They were soon at each other's throats. Bolingbroke decided to retire once more to France to avoid these bitter recriminations, while Pulteney and Carteret even offered to make their peace with Walpole.

Walpole had triumphed over the most formidable and organized opposition he had ever experienced. His position at Court, in the cabinet, and in Parliament appeared more deeply entrenched than ever. The King and Queen wanted him to remain in office, his ministerial colleagues did not openly resist any of his policies, and he was still firmly in control of the Treasury and government patronage. Meanwhile, the opposition in and out of Parliament had begun to crumble. Walpole had once more demonstrated that he was the 'Great Man', whose greed for power barred the advancement of all his rivals. It was his arrogant monopoly of power that drove more and more able men into opposition and eventually revived the campaign against his political and constitutional methods; but for the moment his authority seemed, and indeed was, unchallengeable. His opponents had the dispiriting task of waiting until he blundered again, as he had done over the excise scheme, or until a major crisis developed that would allow them to appeal successfully to the independent backbenchers. Until 1737 neither of these events took place.

Walpole, of course, was never free from one vexatious problem or other. In 1735 his opponents concentrated on attacking the size of the army and navy, which seemed excessive in view of Walpole's boast that he was keeping Britain out of an expensive war in Europe. The Opposition was able to muster very respectable minorities of between 180 and 200 votes, but these were not sufficient to embarrass Walpole. In 1736, Walpole was vexed by serious riots in London and Edinburgh, and by disputes about the privileged position of the Church of England; but the Opposition was unable to exploit these to its advantage. The rioting soon died away, and, besides, Walpole and the Opposition were united in their determination to maintain law and order. The religious disputes probably strengthened Walpole's position. In recent years he had found Bishop Gibson, his ecclesiastical minister, becoming a political liability because of his determination to influence all the promotions within the Church. His stiff-necked attitude brought him into conflict with Lord Chancellor Talbot, Queen Caroline, and Walpole himself. At the same time as this breach with Gibson was widening, Walpole was deciding that it was now expedient to strengthen his majority in the Commons by supporting measures to reduce the privileges of the Church of England. This policy was designed to rally to him the radical Whigs and the Dissenters, who had become somewhat disenchanted with Walpole's earlier opposition to their plans to extend the limits of religious toleration. It would also put Bishop Gibson in his place and might even divide the Opposition along Whig and Tory lines, since their response to such measures would be quite different.

Walpole agreed in 1736 to accept the modest proposal by the Quakers for a Tithe Bill, which would free them from the risk of prosecution in the ecclesiastical courts even though it did not allow them to escape from their liability to pay tithes. Unfortunately, this gesture encouraged the other Dissenters and the radical Whigs to press for the repeal of the Test and Corporation Acts. The introduction of these measures produced alarming demonstrations of anti-Church feeling in Parliament. Walpole feared that matters would get out of hand if he allowed a frontal assault on the Anglican hegemony, for this could well turn the whole Church against him. He therefore decided to vote against the repeal of the Test and Corporation Acts and he saw this measure defeated. Then, having clearly demonstrated his loyalty to the Church of England, he pleased the radical Whigs and Dissenters by letting the Tithe Bill through the Commons. The Opposition was unable to put up much resistance, for while the Tories disliked this measure, the discontented Whigs were reluctant to vote against it. In the Lords, however, Hardwicke and Lord Chancellor Talbot joined fifteen of the bishops in helping to defeat it. These two legal experts argued that the Bill would increase the authority and jurisdiction of J.P.s, who lacked the legal training to deal with complex questions of this nature.

Walpole was prepared to accept the legal advice of his two ministerial colleagues and even the defeat of the Tithe Bill, but he was annoyed that the bishops should take an independent line and attack a bill he had supported in the Commons. He therefore seized this opportunity to teach Edmund Gibson and the other bishops a lesson. Bishop Gibson had made it abundantly clear to Walpole that he would oppose the Tithe Bill even though it had the First Minister's blessing. Not content with voicing his personal objections in private, Gibson decided to lead the bishops in a campaign to persuade the lower clergy to lobby their M.P.s against this measure. Walpole was furious at this open challenge to his authority and was determined that he would never again be humiliated in this way by his ecclesiastical adviser. He made it quite clear to the bishops that Gibson was no longer the ministry's spokesman on church affairs. Ecclesiastical patronage was taken out of the hands of Gibson and handed to the Duke of Newcastle and his more subservient adviser, Bishop Potter. The bishops were left in no doubt where the source of preferment lay and most of them soon deserted Gibson. Though they all disliked the Tithe Bill, eleven bishops abstained rather than vote against the ministry. Thus, Walpole had succeeded in appearing as the friend of the radical Whigs and Dissenters, had divided the Opposition along Whig and Tory lines, and had freed himself from an embarrassing ally. Yet he had also reinforced the Government's control over the hierarchy of the Church. It was a remarkable triumph in a difficult situation. Once again he had demonstrated his unrivalled ability as a political manager. His success only made him more intolerant of those who disagreed with him. He became even more overbearing towards his ministerial colleagues and more ruthless towards his political enemies.

From 1734 to 1736 the Opposition despaired and Walpole seemed at the height of his political career. His colleagues had accepted his decisions without serious criticism and he had even persuaded the King and Queen not to intervene in the War of the Polish Succession when their strong inclination was to support the Emperor. In Parliament the Opposition was more muted than it had been in previous years, and even the campaign against him outside the House, despite the activities of Henry Fielding on the London stage, had temporarily run out of steam. From 1737, however, Walpole began to encounter serious difficulties and considerable resistance. Not all of these problems were of his own making; for example, the death of Queen Caroline and the breach between Prince Frederick and George II were beyond his control. Nor could Walpole have expected the death of his mistress, Maria Skerrett, shortly after he married her in 1738, or the gradual breakdown of his own health. Nevertheless, several of his problems stemmed from the shortsighted nature of some of his earlier policies and the bitterness of the opposition which he had created by his ruthless political tactics. His past conduct began to catch up on him.

In the parliamentary session of 1737 a number of issues came up that enabled Walpole's opponents not only to criticize his particular actions, but to attack his political methods and to accuse him of endangering the constitution. In March 1737 Sir John Barnard, the Opposition's chief spokesman on financial and commercial affairs, laid before the Commons a scheme to reduce the interest rate on the National Debt from 4 per cent to 3 per cent. This proposal was, of course, highly attractive to many Members, particularly the independent country gentlemen, since it would save the nation considerable revenue. Several of Walpole's colleagues, including Newcastle, Henry Pelham, and Horatio Walpole, thought the ministry should accept the scheme; but Walpole feared to disoblige his staunch allies, the great financiers, and opposed the bill. By intense lobbying and by exploiting his financial reputation and expertise to the full, he persuaded the Commons to throw out the proposal in April 1737. Some of his friends believed he had misjudged the issue. He had certainly allowed the Opposition to make out a plausible case that he was prepared to sacrifice the nation's interests in

order to protect the ill-gotten fortunes of a handful of City
financiers.

A month later, in May 1737, Walpole alienated some of
his Scottish supporters and played into the hands of his opponents, when he supported a bill to punish the magistrates and
city of Edinburgh for not preventing the Porteous Riot of the
previous year. This attempt to humiliate the Edinburgh
magistrates and to reduce the privileges of the capital city of
Scotland infuriated nearly all Scots and allowed his opponents
to accuse him of abusing the Government's power in order to
destroy the independence of an important parliamentary constituency. The Duke of Argyll, the greatest peer in Scotland,
went into opposition over this issue. Even his more amenable
brother, the Earl of Islay, who had long been Walpole's political
manager in Scotland, could not support Walpole on this occasion. When the normally docile Scottish Members in the Commons revolted against the ministry, Walpole was forced to
retreat. He wisely allowed the bill to be emasculated of nearly
all its penal clauses, but the ministry never recovered its earlier
dominance over Scottish affairs.

A much more serious blow to Walpole's position and to his
peace of mind was the quarrel between the Prince of Wales
and his parents that came to a head in 1737. Prince Frederick
had long chafed at his lack of independence. He had first quarrelled with his father over whom and when he should marry.
When this disagreement was settled by his marriage in 1736,
the Opposition leaders, anxious to embarrass the Government,
suggested to him that he should press for an increased financial
allowance from the King. George II was always reluctant to
part with money and he resented his son's implicit challenge
to his authority as a father and as a king. His uncompromising
attitude drove his son into the arms of the parliamentary Opposition. In February 1737 the Opposition took up the Prince's cause.
By making it a political rather than a domestic issue, the Opposition forced Walpole to choose between the reigning sovereign
and the heir to the throne. If he came down on the side of the
Prince, he would threaten his own influence at Court, because

the King took the issue very seriously. If he supported George II, he would make Prince Frederick appear a martyr to the King's greed and his decision would cement the tentative alliance between the Prince and the leaders of the Opposition. Walpole's well-developed instinct for political survival made him seek a compromise, but he only succeeded in antagonizing both sides and in splitting the ministry. Some of his younger colleagues, notably Newcastle and Hardwicke, were desperately anxious to remain on good terms with Prince Frederick, for they hoped that they might serve him one day. Though they urged Walpole to find a satisfactory settlement, they could offer him no advice on how to tackle the stubborn King. Walpole therefore had to bear the brunt of the struggle with George II, while he was being continually harassed by his colleagues to make the King come to terms with his son. Although he only gave way after several arguments with his First Minister, George II was eventually persuaded by Walpole to offer his son a more secure allowance of £50,000 per annum. This concession was not enough for the Opposition. Their leaders pressed, on 22 February 1737, for an annual allowance of £100,000. Walpole was forced to defend the King's prerogative to disburse his civil list as he thought fit. His arguments persuaded more than forty Jacobites and Tories to leave the Commons rather than vote to diminish the royal prerogative. Their timely abstention saved Walpole from defeat. After considerable lobbying among his own supporters Walpole only managed to defeat the Opposition's motion by 234 to 204 votes.

Walpole's narrow victory in the Commons was not the end of the matter, for the breach in the royal family had not been healed. Indeed, on 31 July 1737, the Prince deliberately exacerbated the issue by rushing his pregnant wife away from Hampton Court to St James's. He was determined that she would be delivered of her child that night in a palace which was not occupied by the King and Queen. His insulting behaviour incensed the Prince's parents, who decided that their son should be ordered to leave St James's too and live elsewhere. Walpole bowed to their demands, but most of his ministerial colleagues were alarmed at the tone of the message to be delivered to the Prince. The King was clearly accusing him of leading a faction against his Government. Hardwicke led the campaign to per- suade the King to moderate the language of this command to Prince Frederick in order to avoid another political crisis. The style of the letter was altered, but the ministers, after delaying as long as they could, were forced to deliver it. This message finally drove the Prince into a close alliance with the opponents of Walpole. The Opposition now had a respectable figurehead and could no longer be accused of disloyalty to the Hanoverian Settlement. On the other hand, it was in a position to attack Walpole for fomenting this quarrel within the royal family in order to protect his own influence at Court. This charge was not strictly fair, because Walpole had not provoked the final breach. Only when he had been forced to choose sides did he support the King. His colleagues, however, were not convinced that this choice had been necessary and they began to question the wis- dom of Walpole's leadership and policies. His opponents rejoiced at his present embarrassment and at the prospect of overthrow- ing him whenever the Prince should succeed his father. They quite deliberately courted the Prince and set out to praise him as a patriot who would save the constitution from the corrupt methods of Walpole. The old Country programme was revived in a new 'Patriot' guise. The literary critics of Walpole took up their pens to flatter Frederick and to plead the cause of Patriot- ism, while Bolingbroke returned to the political fray by privately circulating among some of the Opposition leaders his treatise on *The Idea of a Patriot King*.

Walpole probably regarded the death of Queen Caroline, on 20 November 1737, as the worst blow that befell him in a very bad year. The Queen had long been Walpole's greatest sup- porter at Court and had helped him to deal with his stubborn and irascible master. In recent years he had disagreed with her over his policy of neutrality in the War of the Polish Succession and he had irritated her by his constant reminders that she must expect her husband to prefer the charms of his young mistress in Hanover. His coarse and tactless references to the declining influence of her physical attractions annoyed her excessively at times, and he found her almost impossible to handle during the disputes with the Prince of Wales. Nevertheless, she did not desert Walpole and, since the King still had a high regard for her political judgement, her support was still valuable. When she fell mortally ill, Walpole feared for his own position at Court and dreaded the political consequences of her demise. Her death did not in fact seriously weaken Walpole's relations with the King, much to the dismay of his political opponents. The King had been irritated by Walpole's conduct during the Queen's last illness, but when, on her death-bed, she recommended her husband to Walpole and Walpole to her husband, both men took her advice to heart. No doubt Walpole did have to work harder to persuade the King to accept his advice, but there is no evidence that he failed more often than in the past. Fortunately, no woman took the Queen's place. The King continued to have his mistresses, but none of them ever matched Caroline's political influence. Walpole's enemies derived little advantage from their intrigues with the royal mistresses or the King's daughters. Nevertheless, the death of the Queen did weaken Walpole's position. He himself lost confidence in his ability to dominate his colleagues. For their part, they could now approach the King direct, without having to combat Caroline's support for Walpole. Certainly, Newcastle and Hardwicke increasingly disagreed with Walpole's conduct of affairs and were prepared to voice their objections at Court. Walpole remained on good terms with the King, but, during his last years in office, he no longer dominated his ministerial colleagues. He gradually lost his grip on government policy.

After a quiet interlude from 1734 to 1736, Walpole experienced more political trouble in 1737 than in any year since the failure of his excise scheme, and perhaps since the furore over the South Sea Bubble. While his influence at Court was not seriously weakened, his authority over his colleagues was gradually undermined. Moreover, the Opposition staged a remarkable revival, and the ministry's majority began to appear vulnerable. Walpole's problems with his colleagues and his opponents were aggravated by the failure of his foreign policy. For some years the South Sea Company and the independent merchants trading with the West Indies had complained about Spain's interference with their legitimate commercial activities. The Government had tried to compose these disputes amicably, but had failed to reach a satisfactory settlement with Spain. The merchant community and public opinion in general became increasingly disenchanted with Walpole's policy and enraged by popular stories of Spanish cruelty. The Opposition skilfully exploited this discontent in order to accuse Walpole of neglecting the country's commercial interests and of sacrificing the country's honour. In 1738 the leaders of the Opposition began to lay before the Commons petitions from merchants complaining against the depredations of the Spanish coastguards in American and West Indian waters. Walpole had to acknowledge that some merchants had legitimate grounds for complaint, especially as Newcastle and Hardwicke were also pressing him to take a firm line with Spain; but he urged the Commons not to pass resolutions which would hamper his attempts to negotiate a settlement. In his efforts to avoid a close investigation of the ministry's recent attempts at negotiating with Spain, he hid behind the royal prerogative to control diplomatic policy and the need to maintain secrecy in such delicate matters. He also endeavoured to amend the Opposition's highly critical motions, because he feared to alienate the independent backbenchers by simply rejecting them.

The chief spokesmen for the Opposition knew that they had Walpole on the defensive and they made every effort to keep up the pressure. Sometimes their conduct was purely factious and opportunistic. Though they pressed Walpole to take a tough line with Spain, they tried to weaken his bargaining position by voting to reduce the size of the standing army. In February 1738, in a very full chamber, they only failed in this attempt by 264 to 249 votes. Walpole, meanwhile, was working furiously to undermine his critics by reaching a settlement with Spain. He appeared to have pulled this off when Britain and Spain signed the Convention of the Pardo in 1739. The Opposition condemned this as unsatisfactory, but the ministry carried it by small majorities through both Houses of Parliament. Walpole was saved from further trouble in this session by the decision of Wyndham and the Tories to leave the Commons in a body, as a protest against the Government's policies. Their Whig allies reluctantly followed them. This dramatic gesture gave some indication of the strength of feeling against the Convention, but, at least temporarily, it let Walpole off the hook. His respite was short-lived, however. The South Sea Company refused to accept the terms of the settlement. When Spain, in turn, began to make difficulties, Walpole's colleagues, particularly Newcastle, argued that it was now impossible to avoid a conflict. In October 1739 Walpole reluctantly bowed to the aggressive mood of the country and declared war on Spain. This decision was greeted with a burst of popular enthusiasm, but Walpole was reported to have observed bitterly: 'They now ring the bells; they will soon wring their hands.'

Walpole survived in power for another two and a half years, but, by agreeing against his better judgement to a declaration of war against Spain, he virtually lost the dominant position he had held for so long. Compelled to fight a war in which he did not believe and increasingly plagued by ill health, he could no longer act as the effectual link between King and Commons. For years he had made himself indispensable to the Crown by his ability to control Parliament. Now Parliament was advocating policies which the King was ready to support, but which he himself disliked. When he failed to conduct the war to the satisfaction of Parliament, his influence gradually waned. The problems posed by the war and the ministry's unpopularity in Parliament naturally provoked discord within the cabinet. Newcastle and Hardwicke, who had been critical of Walpole's policies for some years, were even more impatient with his conduct of the war. There was endless bickering among the leading ministers, with Newcastle and Hardwicke leading the demand for more vigorous action. By 1740 a third ministerial faction had appeared, led by Wilmington and Dorset. This group began to flirt with the Opposition and to undermine the

Government's position even further. Thus Walpole was losing both the confidence of Parliament and the loyalty of his colleagues. He only survived because he retained the support of the King and because there was no agreement on who should replace him or on how to get rid of him.

By declaring war on Spain, Walpole had temporarily cut the ground from under his opponents. The Opposition had to wait until the ministry ran into difficulties over the actual conduct of the war before it could expose Walpole's limitations. In 1740 its leaders concentrated on old issues, bringing forward Place and Pension Bills and criticizing the Convention of the Pardo. William Pulteney and Carteret were more interested in making sure that they would profit from Walpole's difficulties than in co-operating with their Tory allies. Though Walpole was clearly on the defensive, the discontented Whigs and the Tories only succeeded in revealing their own divisions. Their disagreements grew worse after the death of Wyndham in 1740 and as it became apparent that Carteret and Pulteney were only concerned with protecting their own interests. On 13 February 1741, Samuel Sandys, a leading spokesman for the Opposition Whigs, introduced a motion in the Commons to request the King to remove Walpole from office. With the conduct of the war now open to severe criticism, the Whig malcontents believed that they had every justification for this vote of censure. To their surprise and indignation they found little support from their Tory allies. Some Tories were annoyed at not being consulted before the motion was put forward, while others regarded it as an encroachment on the royal prerogative. Many of the independent backbenchers, though disenchanted with Walpole's recent performance in office, had no desire to see him replaced by Pulteney. He would probably continue the same policies but with even less success. They were not prepared to get embroiled in a selfish contest for power. In consequence, the Opposition was hopelessly divided. Some Tories and 'Patriots' voted with Walpole, most of the Opposition Whigs voted against him, while many Tories simply abstained. It was therefore not surprising that the censure motion was defeated; but it was ironic that Walpole should achieve such a major victory when his credit was so low.

The incredible confusion among the ranks of the Opposition prevented any concerted attack on Walpole's inept conduct of the war, but the general election of 1741 finally sounded the death knell of Walpole's long ministry. The failure of the naval war against Spain in the West Indies, and the outbreak of a separate major conflict in Europe that threatened to involve Britain in a Continental war against France, lost Walpole the support of many independent Members and uncommitted voters. His own failings, and not the merits or programme of the Opposition, turned the tide against him. Although he still retained the King's confidence and was again able to exploit the Crown's electoral interest, this was not enough to stem the marked swing of opinion against his administration. He did not actually lose the general election, but his majority was reduced to less than twenty after a keenly contested campaign. He was now highly vulnerable to Opposition attacks. His main electoral reversals were in Cornwall and Scotland, so he clearly paid dearly for his disputes with the Prince of Wales and the Duke of Argyll in 1737. Their electoral influence in these areas alone bit hard into his majority. The Opposition was still not united, but it could at least agree that Walpole should go. Walpole therefore faced a determined Opposition with a reduced majority.

In the first weeks of the new Parliament it became evident that Walpole had a tremendous fight on his hands to demonstrate his ability to manage the Commons. His colleagues had no stomach for a prolonged campaign when the country was facing terrible problems abroad. Two ministerial factions, one led by Newcastle and Hardwicke and the other by Wilmington and Dorset, were ready to sacrifice Walpole and to make overtures to the leaders of the Opposition. When Walpole's fall appeared imminent, even some of the normally loyal members of the Court and Treasury party began to absent themselves from crucial debates in the Commons. They clearly feared to run foul of the Opposition leaders who might soon become their political masters. In the early divisions of the 1741–2 session fortunes swayed between the ministry and the Opposition. Walpole carried a few disputed elections and narrowly defeated an Opposition motion for a committee of inquiry into the conduct of the war. On this vital issue, which was virtually a vote of confidence in his ministry, he carried the day by 253 to 250 votes in a very full House. This was the largest vote ever cast against him and it was obvious he could not long survive against such a formidable Opposition. When he lost by four votes the crucial election of the chairman of the Committee of Privileges and Elections, his friends hoped that this defeat was due to the fact that the ministry's candidate was personally disliked by many backbenchers. This excuse could not account for the ministry's other defeats, particularly over the disputed election for Chippenham. These reverses convinced Walpole that he had lost the confidence of the Commons. After dominating the chamber for more than twenty years it seems ironic that his final defeat should be over such a minor issue as a disputed election; but this was only the occasion and not the cause of his fall. His downfall was really caused by his failure to win the war. When he realized that he had no chance of stemming the tide against him, Walpole decided to abandon the struggle. In February 1742, with obvious reluctance and against the wishes of the King, who was reduced to tears, he resigned all his posts and retired to the Lords as Earl of Orford.

Both the principal and the ultimate cause of Walpole's fall from power was the failure of his foreign policy, which had lost him the support of the independent country gentlemen. His exploitation of crown patronage and his skill in political management had not been enough to retrieve the situation. As the failure of his foreign policy had become increasingly manifest after 1737, Walpole had begun to find his authority challenged on several fronts at once. His old opponents at Court, such as the Earl of Wilmington, had been encouraged to criticize his policies and even his closest cabinet colleagues, such as Newcastle and Hardwicke, who had long been loyal to him, had started to press him to alter his strategy. At the same time the parliamentary Opposition, despite the survival of the old hostility between Whig and Tory factions, had then begun to step up its campaign against Walpole's administration. Nevertheless, the opposition to Walpole at Court, in the cabinet, and in Parliament would not have ended his career in office if the continued failure of his foreign policy had not eventually lost him the votes of many of the independent backbenchers and, thereby, the control of the House of Commons. Walpole never, in fact, forfeited the King's favour, which his bitterest enemies had always regarded as the sole buttress of his authority, but he could not lay claim to it once he was no longer able to serve the King as the effective link between Crown and Parliament, executive and legislature. His success had been based on his ability to make the Revolution Settlement and the balanced constitution work. His fall was dictated by his failure to sustain this essential role of the King's First Minister.

After twenty-one years of power Walpole was at last forced to admit defeat, but he had the satisfaction of denying his enemies a complete triumph. His fall did not signal the collapse of his whole administration, still less of his political system. His old colleagues, Newcastle, Hardwicke, and Henry Pelham, retained the King's favour, remained in office, and continued to command the loyalty of the pro-Government Whigs, the Old Corps. With the political initiative firmly in their hands, they were able to follow Walpole's advice on how to divide the Opposition. They seduced some of the Opposition's leading spokesmen by offering them places in a reconstituted administration, thus encouraging divisions and mutual distrust among the various Opposition groups. Walpole urged them not to trust the Tories, and they themselves feared the political aims of some of the young Patriots, so they concentrated on winning over the Opposition Whigs led by Pulteney and Carteret. It was obvious that these two politicians had no other aim but to gain office. The concessions offered to them, however, were not substantial. Neither of them was to replace Walpole at the head of the Treasury. This important post went to a political nonentity, Spencer Compton, Earl of Wilmington. Carteret had to be content with one of the secretaryships of state, whereas Pulteney's only reward was a peerage. Walpole had advised the King to create his old enemy Earl of Bath in order to reduce his capacity for making trouble for the ministry in the Commons. Not only were Carteret and Pulteney in no position to dominate the new ministry, they were also accused of betraying the principles of the Opposition. Their defection shattered the precarious unity of the anti-Walpole

groups and ensured a parliamentary majority for the reconstituted administration.

By helping to outmanoeuvre and divide his political enemies
Walpole saved himself from prosecution. Before the defection
of Carteret and Pulteney the Opposition had narrowly carried
a motion to appoint a secret committee to inquire into the
conduct of the administration during the last ten years. Henry
Pelham was able to prevent the most virulent antagonists of
Walpole being chosen and even succeeded in getting some Old
Corps Whigs elected to the committee. He was assisted by
Speaker Onslow, who chose the two Members more favourably
disposed towards Walpole when four candidates tied for the
last two vacancies on the committee. Once some of the Opposition leaders began to defect to the Court, the determination to
hound Walpole began to wane. When the committee tried to
investigate Walpole's handling of government contracts and
his interference in elections, it made little headway. Richard
Edgcumbe, who had been one of the ministry's chief electoral
agents, was granted a peerage in order to put him beyond the
reach of the committee. Nicholas Paxton, the Solicitor to the
Treasury, accepted a spell of imprisonment rather than incrimi-
nate his former master, while John Scrope, the Secretary to the
Treasury, adamantly refused to answer any questions. When
the Opposition passed a bill through the Commons to indemnify
those who would come forward with evidence against Walpole,
the Court majority in the Lords threw it out. The committee
laboured on, but it could discover no evidence on which to
frame charges against the former chief minister. It soon became
clear that it would never be able to convict him of corruption.
Walpole was safe to enjoy his retirement in peace.

Walpole was not only safe from the vengeance of his
enemies, but in a position to assist his old colleagues in their
attempts to confound the ambitions of his opponents. Although
he was no longer in office and his ill-health often kept him away
from the Lords, his advice was still eagerly sought and generally
respected by the King and by his political disciple, Henry
Pelham. He continually urged them both to rely on the Old

Corps Whigs and never to trust the Tories or the former Opposition Whigs, even though Carteret and Pulteney (now Earl of
Bath) had been won over. He advised Pelham to retain the support of his former lieutenants in the Commons such as Henry
Fox, Thomas Winnington, and Dudley Ryder. He might even
treat with William Pitt and the Cobhamite faction if they could
be persuaded to support the ministry without seeking to dictate
its policies. Walpole's constant stream of letters to Pelham also
advised him to adopt the same political methods which he had
found so useful during his long administration. Pelham had
already learned much from Walpole about the art of managing
the Commons, for he had been one of his chief lieutenants since
1724. Walpole now reminded him of the need to keep in touch
with the Whigs by summoning regular meetings at the Cockpit
and of the wisdom of drawing up the King's Speech before the
opening of each session of Parliament. In 1743 he instructed
Pelham on the value of being at the head of the Treasury,
because this position would put him in charge of financial affairs,
at the centre of the whole network of government patronage,
and in frequent contact with the King. No other post could offer
so many political advantages. No office was more vital for
managing the King and the Commons. Therefore, when the
Earl of Wilmington, the First Lord of the Treasury, died in 1743,
Walpole urged Pelham to fill the vacancy himself. At all costs
he must prevent the Earl of Bath succeeding to it. When Pelham
accepted the responsibility of this vital office, Walpole was
delighted. His political disciple was now the strongest individual
in the ministry and he was in the best possible position for
thwarting Carteret's attempts to dominate the Government's
policies.

Carteret, as soon as he had become Secretary of State, had
endeavoured to dictate the ministry's foreign policy. His knowledge of German and his concern for the interests of Hanover
endeared him to the King, but his ambitious and expensive
diplomatic manoeuvres in Europe alarmed his colleagues in the
ministry. Walpole warned Pelham and Newcastle not to alienate
George II by pressing too far with their objections to Carteret's

policies, particularly to the notion of having Hanoverian troops in British pay. The Pelhams must learn the arts of court intrigue at least as well as Carteret. They must follow Walpole's own example of letting the King believe that he was making the decisions when, in fact, he was accepting advice. By making himself acceptable to the King while also demonstrating that he had won the confidence of the Commons, Henry Pelham would make himself indispensable and eventually he would be able to outmanoeuvre Carteret. The King would learn that Carteret could make many promises, but only Pelham could get things done. Henry Pelham followed Walpole's advice so well that when, in November 1744, he and Carteret finally fell out about the conduct of the War of the Austrian Succession, he was in the stronger position. Carteret had the King's support for his Hanoverian policies, but only Pelham could raise the supplies needed to fight the war, and only Pelham had the support of the Commons. The unhappy King, reluctant to lose Carteret, appealed to Walpole, who advised him to accept the views of Pelham and Newcastle. Carteret was forced to resign, and once more Walpole had triumphed over his old enemies. For the next ten years Henry Pelham was entrenched in power. Stable government had returned once Pelham had grasped all the reasons for Walpole's political success. Thereafter, the ministry's policies and methods were modelled on those of Walpole.

His support for Pelham in November 1744 was Walpole's last intervention in national affairs. Early in 1745 he fell seriously ill, suffering from stones in the kidney and internal haemorrhages. He was given repeated doses of opium to help him cope with the pain, but his doctors did more harm than good by their efforts to cure him. His strong constitution kept him alive for several weeks, but he finally succumbed on 18 March. Although his son claimed that he died in debt, Walpole in fact left enormous assets, including a magnificent palace, a huge art collection, and large estates. He also left all his family holding lucrative places and pensions under the Crown. Walpole earned these rewards, however, for he left his Whig successors a great political inheritance. His life's work, the stability of the

Hanoverian succession and the Revolution Settlement, was menaced by another Jacobite rebellion later in 1745, but Walpole had clearly not laboured in vain. The political structure and the Whig constitution survived both this threat and the consequences of an unsuccessful war against France and Spain. Walpole's constitutional principles and his political techniques served as the model for all the other successful ministers of the eighteenth century. They professed the same aims: the stability of the Hanoverian succession, the Revolution Settlement, and the Whig supremacy. They practised many of the same methods: the combination of court intrigue, government patronage, and parliamentary management. Such aims and methods became a familiar feature of all successful administrations in the eighteenth century, but Walpole was the first minister to demonstrate their effectiveness. Above all else, he made the political system work and achieved domestic harmony.

Bibliography

The place of publication is London unless otherwise stated

PRIMARY SOURCES

1. *Manuscripts*:   The most valuable unpublished Walpole papers
are the Cholmondeley (Houghton) MSS deposited in Cambridge
University Library. There are many other unpublished Walpole
letters in the British Museum, particularly among the Newcastle
papers (notably Add MSS 32686–701, 32786 and 33034), but also in
Add MS 35335 and Stowe MS 251. There are useful Walpole letters
among the Erle papers in Churchill College Library, Cambridge; the
Marlborough papers at Blenheim Palace (B 1 and B 2); in MS 274 in
Chicago University Library; and in the Norfolk and Norwich Record
Office. There are a few Walpole letters in State Papers Domestic 35
and 36 at the Public Record Office; Henry E. Huntington Library,
California; Nottingham University Library; Pierpont Morgan
Library, New York; and Yale University Library.
2. *Printed*:   Many valuable Walpole letters from private collec-
tions are published in Volumes 2 and 3 of William Coxe's *Memoirs
of the Life and Administration of Sir Robert Walpole* (3 vols., 1798)
and some useful letters in two other works by William Coxe,
Memoirs of Horatio, Lord Walpole (2 vols., 3rd ed., 1820) and
Memoirs of the Administration of Henry Pelham (2 vols., 1829).
Other letters of interest are printed in *Letters and Dispatches of
Marlborough*, ed. Sir George Murray (5 vols., 1845); P. C. Yorke, *The
Life and Correspondence of Philip Yorke, Earl of Hardwicke* (3 vols.,
Cambridge, 1913); *Letters of Philip Dormer Stanhope, Fourth Earl of
Chesterfield*, ed. Bonamy Dobrée (6 vols., 1932); *The Yale Edition of
Horace Walpole's Correspondence*, ed. W. S. Lewis and others
(1937–); and in Historical Manuscripts Commission *Carlisle MSS,
Mar and Kellie MSS, Polwarth MSS*, Vol. v, *Portland MSS*, Vols. v and

vii, *Stuart MSS*, Vols. iv and v, and *14th Report*, App. Pt. ix (Hare, Onslow, and Trevor MSS). There is a great deal about Walpole in the four major sources for the politics of this period: Hist. MSS Comm., *Egmont Diary* (3 vols.); *Some Materials Towards Memoirs of the Reign of King George II, by John, Lord Hervey*, ed. Romney Sedgwick (3 vols., 1931); *The Parliamentary Diary of Sir Edward Knatchbull 1722–1730*, ed. A. N. Newman (Camden Soc., 1963); Vol. xciv; and William Cobbett's *Parliamentary History of England*, Vols. 6–12. Less valuable, but still useful, are the *Diary of Mary, Countess Cowper*, ed. Spencer Compton (1864); Peter, Lord King, *The Life of John Locke*, App. Vol. 2 (1830); Horace Walpole, *Walpoliana* (1783); *Characters of Eminent Personages of His Own Time, written by the late Earl of Chesterfield* (1777); and *Political Ballads illustrating the administration of Sir Robert Walpole*, ed. Milton Percival (Oxford, 1916).

SECONDARY SOURCES

1. General: The best complete biography of Walpole is still the first volume of William Coxe's *Memoirs of the Life and Administration of Sir Robert Walpole* (1798), though J. H. Plumb is two-thirds of the way through a modern standard-life, *Sir Robert Walpole* (2 vols., 1956, 1960). The biographies published between the works of Coxe and Plumb have little to commend them. F. S. Oliver, *The Endless Adventure* (3 vols., 1930–5) is of greater value, though not a biography. The entry in the *Dictionary of National Biography* is a sound, though short biography. For the general political background of Walpole's career, see Geoffrey Holmes, *British Politics in the Age of Anne* (1967); H. T. Dickinson, *Bolingbroke* (1970); J. H. Plumb, *The Growth of Political Stability in England 1675–1725* (1967); J. H. Plumb, *England in the Eighteenth Century* (1950); Dorothy Marshall, *Eighteenth Century England* (1962); Basil Williams, *The Whig Supremacy* (Oxford, 2nd ed., 1962); W. T. Laprade, *Public Opinion and Politics in the Eighteenth Century* (New York, 1936); A. S. Turberville, *The House of Lords in the XVIIIth Century* (Oxford, 1927); Lewis Namier, *The Structure of Politics at the Accession of George III* (2nd ed., 1957); and *The House of Commons 1715–1754*, ed. Romney Sedgwick (2 vols., 1970).
2. Walpole's Earlier Career: J. H. Plumb, 'The Walpoles: Father and Son', in *Men and Places* (1963) and 'Sir Robert Walpole and Norfolk Husbandry', *Econ. Hist. Rev.* (1952); and E. R. Turner, 'The Peerage Bill of 1719', *Eng. Hist. Rev.* (1913).

3. *Walpole's Political Management*:   Much has to be culled from the major primary sources noted above, particularly *Lord Hervey's Memoirs, Egmont Diary, Knatchbull Diary*, and Cobbett's *Parliamentary History*. See also, P. D. G. Thomas, *The House of Commons in the Eighteenth Century* (Oxford, 1971); J. M. Beattie, *The English Court in the reign of George I* (Cambridge, 1967); J. Steven Watson, 'Arthur Onslow and Party Politics' in *Essays in British History presented to Sir Keith Feiling*, ed. H. R. Trevor-Roper (1964); R. R. Sedgwick, 'The Inner Cabinet from 1739 to 1741', *Eng. Hist. Rev.* (1919); S. H. Nulle, 'The Duke of Newcastle and the Election of 1727', *Journal of Modern History* (1937); Basil Williams, 'The Duke of Newcastle and the Election of 1734', *Eng. Hist. Rev.* (1897); A. Goodwin, 'Wood's Halfpence', *Eng. Hist. Rev.* (1936); P. W. J. Riley, *The English Ministers and Scotland 1707–1727* (1964); Norman Sykes, *Edmund Gibson, Bishop of London* (Oxford, 1926); N. C. Hunt, 'Sir Robert Walpole, Samuel Holden, and the Dissenting Deputies', *Friends of Dr Williams's Library*, 11th Lecture (1957); and T. F. J. Kendrick, 'Sir Robert Walpole, the Old Whigs and the Bishops 1733–1736', *Historical Journal* (1968).

4. *Walpole's Financial and Commercial Policies*:   Hubert Hall, 'The Sources for the History of Sir Robert Walpole's Financial Administration', *Trans. Royal Hist. Soc.* (1910); N. A. Brisco, *The Economic Policy of Robert Walpole* (New York, 1907); P. G. M. Dickson, *The Financial Revolution in England* (1967); E. R. Turner, 'The Excise Scheme of 1733', *Eng. Hist. Rev.* (1927); Ralph Davis, 'The Rise of Protection in England 1689–1786', *Econ. Hist. Rev.* (1966); John G. Sperling, *The South Sea Company* (Boston, Mass., 1962); John Carswell, *The South Sea Bubble* (1960); E. L. Hargreaves, *The National Debt* (1930); William Kennedy, *English Taxation 1640–1799* (1913); Edward Hughes, *Studies in Administration and Finance* (Manchester, 1934); G. B. Hertz, 'England and the Ostend Company', *Eng. Hist. Rev.* (1907); and N. C. Hunt, 'The Russia Company and the Government 1730–1742', *Oxford Slavonic Papers* (1957).

5. *Walpole's Foreign Policy*:   G. C. Gibbs, 'The Revolution in Foreign Policy' in *Britain after the Glorious Revolution 1689–1714*, ed. Geoffrey Holmes (1969); G. C. Gibbs, 'Parliament and Foreign Policy in the Age of Stanhope and Walpole', *Eng. Hist. Rev.* (1962); G. C. Gibbs, 'Newspapers, Parliament, and Foreign Policy in the Age of Stanhope and Walpole', in *Mélanges offerts à G. Jacquemyns* (Brussels, 1968); G. C. Gibbs, 'Britain and the Alliance of Hanover,

April 1725 – February 1726', *Eng. Hist. Rev.* (1958); Richard Lodge, 'The Anglo-French Alliance 1716–31' in *Studies in Anglo-French History*, ed. A. Coville and H. Temperley (Cambridge, 1935); Richard Lodge, 'The Treaty of Seville, 1729', *Trans. Royal Hist. Soc.* (1933); Richard Lodge, 'English Neutrality in the War of the Polish Succession', *Trans. Royal Hist. Soc.* (1931); Basil Williams, 'Walpole's Foreign Policy', six articles in *Eng. Hist. Rev.* (1900–1); J. F. Chance, 'The Treaty of Charlottenberg', *Eng. Hist. Rev.* (1912); H. W. V. Temperley, 'The Causes of the War of Jenkins' Ear 1739', *Trans. Royal Hist. Soc.* (1909); *British Diplomatic Instructions*, Vols. iv and vi, *France 1721–27 and 1727–44*, ed. L. G. Wickham Legg (Camden Soc., 1927 and 1931); Paul Vaucher, *Robert Walpole et la Politique de Fleury, 1732–42* (Paris, 1924); A. M. Wilson, *French Foreign Policy during the Administration of Cardinal Fleury, 1726–1743* (Cambridge, Mass., 1936); and Richard Pares, *War and Trade in the West Indies 1739–1763* (Oxford, 1936).

6. *Walpole and the Opposition*:   C. B. Realey, *The Early Opposition to Sir Robert Walpole, 1720–1727* (Philadelphia, 1931); A. S. Foord, *His Majesty's Opposition, 1714–1830* (Oxford, 1964); H. T. Dickinson, *Bolingbroke* (1970); Isaac Kramnick, *Bolingbroke and His Circle* (Oxford, 1968); David H. Stevens, *Party Politics and English Journalism 1702–1742* (Menasha, Wisconsin, 1916); Lawrence Hanson, *Government and the Press 1695–1763* (Oxford, 1936); John B. Owen, *The Rise of the Pelhams* (1957); Paul Vaucher, *La Crise du Ministère Walpole en 1733–1734* (Paris, 1924); A. J. Henderson, *London and the National Government 1721–1742* (Durham, N. Carolina, 1945); Lucy Sutherland, 'The City of London in Eighteenth Century Politics', in *Essays presented to Sir Lewis Namier*, ed. R. Pares and A. J. P. Taylor (1956); John Loftis, *The Politics of Augustan Drama* (Oxford, 1963); Maynard Mack, *The Garden and the City* (1969); Peter Dixon, *The World of Pope's Satires* (1968); John Butt, 'Pope and the Opposition to Walpole's Government', in *Pope, Dickens and Others: Essays and Addresses by John Butt*, ed. G. Carnall (Edinburgh, 1969); Phyllis Hartnoll, 'The Theatre and the Licensing Act of 1737', in *Silver Renaissance*, ed. Alex Natan (1961); John Hardy, 'Johnson's London: The Country versus the City', in *Studies in the Eighteenth Century*, ed. R. F. Brissenden (Canberra, 1968); and E. L. Avery and A. H. Scouten, 'The Opposition to Sir Robert Walpole 1737–1739', *Eng. Hist. Rev.* (1968).

Index

Index

Orford, 77
Orford, Edward Russell, 1st Earl
    of, 16
Orleans, Philippe, Duke of, 118,
    162
Ormonde, James Butler, 2nd
    Duke of, 30, 48
Orrery, Charles Boyle, 4th Earl
    of, 158
Ostend East India Company, 110,
    121, 122, 123, 130, 168
Ottoman Turk, 120, 123
Oxenden, Sir George, 81, 144
Oxford University, 76

Page, Sir Francis, 78
Pardo, Convention of the, 136,
    182, 183, 184
Paris, 122, 162, 168
Parma, 119, 126, 127, 129–30, 134
Pasquin, 143
Patriots, 151, 157, 180, 184
Paxton, Nicholas, 189
Peerage Bill, 52–3
Pelham, Henry, 65, 72, 76, 83, 84,
    164, 168, 170, 177, 188–91
Peter the Great, Tsar of Russia,
    121
Philip V of Spain, 119
Piacenza, 126, 127, 129–30, 134
Pitt, William, 190
Place and Pension Bills, 80, 87,
    148, 157, 167, 184
Platen, Countess von, 162
Plumb, J. H., 56
Plymouth, 77
Poland, 123, 132–4
Polly, 156
Pope, Alexander, 140, 141, 143,
    144, 146, 151
Porteous riot in Edinburgh, 90,
    174, 178
Porto Bello, 138
Portsmouth, 77
Potter, Bishop John, 176
Pragmatic Sanction, 120, 130, 131,
    134, 135
Pretender, James Edward Stuart,

the, 23, 27, 30, 34, 37, 48, 52,
    83, 118, 119, 157, 158, 164
Prussia, 119, 121, 122, 138, 139
Pulteney, William, later Earl of
    Bath, 17, 39, 42, 49, 55, 65,
    72, 83, 115, 140, 147, 149,
    150, 157, 158, 164, 166, 172,
    174, 184, 188–90

Quakers, 92, 175–6

Realey, C. B., 56
Revolution Settlement, 14–16, 19,
    29, 30, 32, 40, 44, 83, 148, 151,
    153, 172, 187, 191
Robethon, Jean, 113
Robin will be out at last, 143
Robinson, Thomas, 128, 168
Rochester, 77
Roxburgh, John Ker, 1st Duke of,
    72, 163
Russia, 119, 121, 132, 133, 138, 162
Russia Company, 111, 112
Rutland, John Manners, 3rd Duke
    of, 77
Ryder, Dudley, 72, 190

Sacheverell, Dr Henry, 28–30
St Quinten, Sir William, 49
salt duty, 75, 95, 97, 168
Sandys, Samuel, 166, 186
Sardinia, 133
Scarborough, Richard Lumley, 1st
    Earl of, 169, 171
Schism Act (1714), 38, 52
Scotland, 25, 72, 73, 77, 90, 97,
    163, 178, 185
Scrope, John, 75, 84, 95, 173, 189
Secret Service Fund, 64, 78
Septennial Act (1716), 41, 48, 148,
    158, 172
Seville, Treaty of, 115, 116, 127,
    128, 129, 130, 167
Shawfield riot, 72, 163
Sherlock, Thomas, 77
Shippen, William, 41, 90, 149, 157
Shorter, Catherine, 12–13